2026

ULTIMATE FOOTBALL HEROES

First published by Dino Books in 2025,
an imprint of Bonnier Books UK,
5th Floor, HYLO, 105 Bunhill Row,
London, EC1Y 8LZ
www.bonnierbooks.co.uk

X @UFHbooks
X @footieheroesbks
www.heroesfootball.com

Text © Studio Press 2025

All rights reserved. No part of this publication may be reproduced, stored in a
retrieval system, or transmitted in any form or by any means, without the prior
permission in writing of the publisher, nor be otherwise circulated in any form
of binding or cover other than that in which it is published and without a similar
condition including this condition being imposed on the subsequent purchaser.

Paperback ISBN: 978 1 78946 902 8
E-book ISBN: 978 1 78946 923 3

Written by Matt Oldfield, Emily Stead, Seth Burkett and John Murray
Edited by Tolly Maggs
Design by Alessandro Susin
Cover illustrations by Dan Leydon
Production by Natalie Tang

British Library cataloguing-in-publication data:
A catalogue record for this book is available from the British Library.

3 5 7 9 10 8 6 4 2

MIX
Paper | Supporting
responsible forestry
FSC® C013604

All names and trademarks are the property of their respective owners,
which are in no way associated with Dino Books. Use of these
names does not imply any cooperation or endorsement.

Printed and bound by CPI (UK) Ltd, Croydon CR0 4YY

The authorised representative in the EEA is Bonnier Books UK (Ireland) Limited.
Registered office address:
Block B, The Crescent Building
Northwood, Santry
Dublin 9, D09 C6X8, Ireland
compliance@bonnierbooks.ie

2026

ULTIMATE FOOTBALL HEROES

Matt Oldfield

Emily Stead

Seth Burkett

John Murray

INTRODUCTION

Welcome to Ultimate Football Heroes 2026 – the new annual round-up of the most exciting stories from a thrilling season of the beautiful game!

Matt Oldfield keeps up the pace with every twist and turn of the Premier League, featuring Man City, Arsenal, Chelsea and Liverpool. Emily Stead then recaps every thrilling moment of the Lionesses thundering up the goals all the way up to a thrilling women's Euro's finale.

John Murray neatly heads in a series of all the biggest glories from the European cups, plus all the best action from the big leagues in France, Germany, Spain, Italy and Scotland.

And Seth Burkett brings in the best of the best as we select the best goals, players, teams and much more from around the world of football.

Then you can test what you've learned and prove to be the ultimate football fan with our annual quiz and activities. Search and discover in our word search, solve crafty puzzles the football themed anagrams, and so much more in our adventurous activity section.

The fans are howling... the players are in position... Let's blow the whistle on Ultimate Football Heroes 2026!

MEET THE AUTHORS

Matt Oldfield is a children's author focusing on the wonderful world of football. His other books include *Unbelievable Football* (winner of the 2020 Children's Sports Book of the Year) and the *Johnny Ball: Football Genius* series. In association with his writing, Matt also delivers writing workshops in schools.

Seth Burkett is an author, ghostwriter and former professional footballer. Having played in Brazil and Sri Lanka, Seth now dedicates his time to writing and speaking in schools. He has published 16 books, including *Tekkers* and *The Football GOAT* series.

Emily Stead has loved writing for children ever since she was a child herself! Working as a children's writer and editor, she has created books about some of football's biggest stars, teams and tournaments for many a season. When she's not writing, you can probably find her watching from the sidelines at her youngest son's matches or attempting to play the beautiful game herself in Yorkshire.

John Murray has written and edited books on a wide range of sports, from football and fencing to tennis and Test cricket. He is the content director at Touchline.

TABLE OF CONTENTS

ENGLISH PREMIER LEAGUE – MATT & TOM OLDFIELD.....1

★ TOP 5 YOUNG PLAYERS – SETH BURKETT.............91

WOMEN'S SUPER LEAGUE – EMILY STEAD.............97

★ TOP 5 TEAM PERFORMANCES – SETH BURKETT.......140

WOMEN'S EUROS 2025 – EMILY STEAD.............147

★ TOP 5 INDIVIDUAL PERFORMANCES – SETH BURKETT..154

EUROPA LEAGUE – JOHN MURRAY..................161

★ TOP 5 TEAMS – SETH BURKETT....................170

EUROPA CONFERENCE LEAGUE – JOHN MURRAY.......177

★ TOP 5 GOALS – SETH BURKETT...................186

SERIE A – JOHN MURRAY........................193

★ TOP 5 GAMES – SETH BURKETT...................202

BUNDESLIGA – JOHN MURRAY.....................211

- ★ **TOP 5 SIGNINGS – SETH BURKETT** 222
- **LA LIGA – JOHN MURRAY** 231
- ★ **TOP 5 MANAGERS – SETH BURKETT** 242
- **LIGUE 2 – JOHN MURRAY** 249
- ★ **TOP 5 CRAZIEST MOMENTS – SETH BURKETT** 258
- **SCOTTISH PREMIER LEAGUE – JOHN MURRAY** 265
- ★ **TOP 5 INCREDIBLE MOMENTS – SETH BURKETT** 274
- **CHAMPIONS LEAGUE – JOHN MURRAY** 283
- ★ **TOP 5 PLAYERS – SETH BURKETT** 292
- **ACTIVITIES** 300
- **ANSWERS** 322

ENGLISH PREMIER LEAGUE

PART ONE

SAKA
FIGHTING TO FINISH FIRST

As his 2023–24 season finally came to an end, Bukayo was filled with a mix of powerful emotions. On a personal level, he felt deeply proud of the progress he'd made, and the extra goals he'd added to his game. For club, he'd finished as Arsenal's top scorer across all competitions, and for country, he'd been one of England's heroes at Euro 2024, especially in the quarter-finals against Switzerland. After curling in a beautiful equaliser, Bukayo had then put his previous penalty pain at Euro 2020 behind him by scoring in the shoot-out too!

But despite all his big moments, there was one very important thing missing: a team trophy. Yes, for the second Premier League season in a row, Arsenal had just come second behind Manchester City, and for the second Euros in a row, England had just lost in the final, this time against Spain.

Noooooo, not again! Was Bukayo destined to be a runner-up forever? It certainly felt that way when he trudged off the pitch in despair after the Euro 2024 final, but a well-deserved holiday – or a 'Rest & Reset' as he called it on social media – soon got him thinking more positively again. And by the time he returned to Arsenal in early August 2024, Bukayo was feeling hungrier than ever.

'Come on, we've *gotta* make this our year!' he kept telling his teammates while they prepared for the new Premier League season.

Although Bukayo had said goodbye and good luck to two of his best friends from the club's academy – Emile Smith Rowe and Eddie Nketiah – overall, the Arsenal squad was stronger than before. New Italian defender Riccardo Calafiori looked slick at left-back or centre-back, while Mikel Merino was an excellent, all-round midfielder who had starred for Spain at Euro

2024. Sure, another sharp-shooting striker would have been useful to get more goals up front, but never mind, Arsenal had plenty of other scoring options...

On the opening day of the season against Wolves, Bukayo got the ball wide on the right wing, looked up, and delivered a perfect left-foot cross onto Kai Havertz's head. *1–0!*

Then when things got tense in the second half, it was Bukayo who sealed the victory with a curling strike into the bottom corner. *2–0!*

Goooooooooooooooooooooooaaaaaaaaaaaaaaaaaaaaaaaaalllllllllllllllllllllllll!

As he celebrated in front of the Arsenal fans at the Emirates, Bukayo threw his arms out wide with a smile and a shrug. What else did they expect from their beloved Starboy?

A goal, an assist, and a first win of the season – with Bukayo on fire already, the fight was on to finish first in the Premier League. But as brilliant as he was, he wasn't Arsenal's only attacking superstar – under manager Mikel Arteta, the goals were always shared around the team.

ENGLISH PREMIER LEAGUE

Leandro Trossard and Thomas Partey were the scorers in their 2–0 win at Aston Villa, then Kai in the 1–1 draw with Brighton...

...defender Gabriel Magalhães in the North London derby victory over Tottenham...

...and Riccardo and Gabriel Magalhães in the 2–2 draw at Manchester City.

But who set up their crucial goal in each of those games? That's right, Bukayo – he had five assists in his first five games of the season!

At the age of only 22, Bukayo had become such a key part of the Arsenal team that when Martin Ødegaard was ruled out with a serious ankle injury, Arteta decided to make Bukayo captain for the matches against Manchester City and Leicester City. A 2–2 draw and a 4–2 win resulted – hurray, his leadership career was off to a strong start!

In their next game against Southampton, Jorginho wore the armband, but Bukayo was still the player who inspired Arsenal to victory. When his team went 1–0 down early in the second half, he reacted instantly, working hard to win the ball back and then quickly playing it forward to Kai. *1–1!*

'That's more like it – come onnnnnnn!' Bukayo cried out with passion, grabbing the ball out of the net and racing back for the restart. Because a draw wouldn't do; if they were going to finish first and win the Premier League title, Arsenal needed to win as many games as possible, and Bukayo was determined to keep fighting until he achieved his goal.

Ten minutes later, he set up Gabriel Martinelli with an incredible cross to the back post, and before the final whistle blew, Bukayo pounced on a Southampton mistake to make it 3–1. Job done – with a goal and two assists, he had successfully secured all three points for his team!

'He's unbelievable, one of the best players in the world right now,' Gabriel Martinelli admiringly said of Bukayo after the match. Yes, and what on earth would Arsenal do without him? They sorely missed his absence, due to a thigh problem, in the next match when they lost 2–0 at Bournemouth!

But at least Bukayo was back a week later for their top-of-the-table clash with Liverpool. In the ninth minute, he raced onto Ben White's amazing long ball, cut inside past Andrew Robertson, and then whipped a shot past Caoimhín Kelleher. *1–0!*

Gooooooooooooooooooooooaaaaaaaaaaaaaaaaaaaaaa aaaaallllllllllllllllllllllllllllll!

Bukayo had just become the youngest player ever to score 50 times in the Premier League, but while the Arsenal supporters went wild all around him, he as captain stayed calm and just shrugged. Banging in big-game goals – easy, what else did they expect from their beloved Starboy?

'Yessssss, you're the best, B!' Kai cheered, throwing his arms around their hero.

The match wasn't over yet, though. Twice, Liverpool came back to equalise, and so it ended 2–2 at the Emirates.

'Argh, we should have won that!' Bukayo groaned in frustration. It was Arsenal's third draw in their first nine games, compared with only five in the whole of the previous season.

But while he was bitterly disappointed, Bukayo refused to let it get him down for long. After all, a draw was always better than a defeat in football, and Arsenal were still right in the title race: four points behind Liverpool, and five behind the leaders Manchester City.

Plus, they still had plenty of games to go, starting with a tricky trip to Newcastle United. . .

ISAK
BACK TO HIS BEST

2 November 2024, St James' Park, Newcastle

'. . . And Number 14 Alexander ISAAAAAAAAK!'

When his name was announced, an almighty roar rang out around the stadium. Hurray – Newcastle's club record signing was starting up front in their big game against Arsenal! And hopefully, after a slow start to the season, Alexander was getting back to his lethal best.

During the 2023–24 campaign, Alexander had been sensational, scoring 21 Premier League goals, including 11 in his last 12 games. The Newcastle fans had fallen in love with him, thinking they had finally found their 'next Alan Shearer', a superstar striker who could win them trophies and fire the club back into the Champions League. In their first eight league matches of the 2024–25 season, however, the Swede had only scored once.

Oh dear – was Alexander going to be a one-year wonder, after all? No, no, there was no need to start panicking yet. He had missed two of those eight matches because of a broken toe, and it wasn't as if he was the only Newcastle player struggling to find form; so were all of their other attackers! Without a single win in their last five games, the team had slumped all the way down to 12th place in the table.

Plus, for Alexander there was also a lot of uncertainty over whether the club would offer him a new contract, or look to sell him for a huge amount of money instead. He had tried his best not to let the talk affect his performances on the pitch, but it wasn't easy.

'I want Alex to be focused on football,' his manager, Eddie Howe, had said ahead of Newcastle's ninth league game against Chelsea. 'My main job at the moment is to get Alex fit and playing his best football, enjoying his best football and scoring goals.'

Challenge accepted! Alexander had successfully found the net against Chelsea, and once he started scoring, he usually couldn't stop. . .

DANGER ALERT!

Against Arsenal, however, Alexander would be up against William Saliba and Gabriel Magalhães, two of the best centre-backs in not just the Premier League, but the whole world. Would he be able to keep both of them busy with his pace, power, and quick, clever movement?

'Bring it on!' Alexander thought to himself, calmly walking forward for kick-off.

The first good chance of the game fell to Arsenal's Number 7, Bukayo Saka, but his shot flew just wide of the post. And the second? To Newcastle's Number 14!

In the 11th minute, the ball dropped at Alexander's feet just outside the Arsenal box, and he controlled it brilliantly, turned, and then played a short pass across to Sean Longstaff, who spread the ball wide to Anthony Gordon on the right wing, who whipped a fantastic, first-time cross into the middle for. . . Alexander!

Yes, he had continued his run into the box, in between the two Arsenal centre-backs, and as the cross came in, he used his height and athleticism to jump high above Gabriel Magalhães and power the ball towards the top corner. . .

Alexander was better known for his skilful feet and

accurate shooting, but this was an unstoppable header that even Shearer himself would have been proud of...

Goooooooooooooooooooooooaaaaaaaaaaaaaaaaaaaa aaaaalllllllllllllllllllllllllllll!

Yesssssssss, Newcastle's new superstar striker was officially back with a *BOOM!* Alexander celebrated with a knee slide like he usually did, and then got up and gave Anthony a big hug to say thanks. Together, they had just put the Toon Army 1–0 up against Arsenal!

Once the last of his teammates had left him, Alexander turned to the fans and raised and dropped his arms up and down, urging them to make even more noise. 'Come onnnnnnnnnnnn!' he cried out, punching the air with passion.

And how did the Newcastle supporters respond? By singing their special song for him at the top of their voices:

Gimme gimme gimme a striker from Sweden,
He's our Number 14 and he plays in attack.
Gimme gimme gimme a striker from Sweden,
First name's Alexander and his surname's Isak!

What a tune, and what a feeling! Alexander could have stood there soaking up the amazing St James' Park atmosphere for hours, but he had lots more work to do, in defence as well as attack. His team had the lead, but could they hold on for a vital victory?

It took a huge team effort – with Alexander and Anthony pressing from the front, Sean and captain Bruno Guimarães battling for every ball in midfield, and Dan Burn and Fabian Schär keeping out Saka and co. at the back – but together, they got the job done. Eventually, the final whistle blew, and Newcastle were the winners.

'VAMOOOOOOOOSSS!' roared Joelinton, sharing a big high-ten and chest bump with their goalscoring hero. Alexander, however, wasn't the type of person who got too carried away. So, while he walked around the pitch, smiling and swapping handshakes and hugs, he looked as cool and calm as ever. A brilliant header to beat Arsenal? No big deal!

But while the win only lifted Newcastle up one place in the Premier League table – from 12th to 11th – it felt much more significant than that to the players. It felt like a turning point in their frustrating season so far, and hopefully the start of a better run of form.

'That was massive, a big game against a big team, it means a lot,' a tired Alexander said in his post-match TV interview. 'We've had a bad spell but hopefully this win will be an ice-breaker for us.'

With their superstar striker back to his lethal best, things were finally looking up for Newcastle United.

SALAH
ON FIRE FROM THE START

Meanwhile over at Liverpool, new manager Arne Slot was off to the perfect start. Most people had expected the team to need time to adapt to the Dutchman's new tactics, but so far, the Reds were flying high at the top of the Premier League table!

It certainly helped that the Liverpool squad hadn't really changed since the 2023–24 season. Other than one new signing, Italian forward Federico Chiesa, and one switch of position – with Dutch maestro Ryan Gravenberch moving deeper into the Number 6 defensive midfield role – it was the same strong, settled group of guys who had been playing together for a while:

Alisson in goal, Trent Alexander-Arnold, Virgil van Dijk, Ibrahima Konaté and Andy Robertson in defence, Alexis Mac Allister, Curtis Jones and Dominik Szoboszlai in midfield. . .

. . . and in attack, Luis Díaz, Diogo Jota, Cody Gakpo, Darwin Núñez, and of course Liverpool's main man, Mohamed Salah!

At the age of 32, some argued that Mo's best Premier League days were now behind him, but the man they called 'The Egyptian King' disagreed, and so did his super-consistent stats:

Season	Goals	Assists
2021–22	31	15
2022–23	30	16
2023–24	25	14

So, what about 2024–25? Well, after a relaxing summer break, Mo came back to England determined to show that he was still one of the most dangerous attackers around, and right from the very start of the new season, he was on fire.

In Liverpool's opening game against Ipswich Town, Mo set up the first for Diogo, and then scored the second himself. *ASSIST! GOAL!*

A week later against Brentford, he steered a classy left-foot finish around the keeper. *GOAL!*

And away at Old Trafford against Liverpool's big rivals Manchester United, Mo was even more impressive, providing two assists for Luis, followed by a killer, bottom-corner finish of his own.

Goooooooooooooooooooooooaaaaaaaaaaaaaaaaaaaa aaaaalllllllllllllllllllllllllll!

There was just no stopping Mo at the moment, and it was time for another showing of his new 'archer' celebration. After pretending to take an arrow from the quiver, he pulled back his bowstring and *PING!* off the arrow flew towards the target, just like one of his shots.

But after the win, it wasn't Mo's performance that everyone was talking about; it was his post-match interview. 'As you know, this is my last year with the club and I want to enjoy it,' he told the TV reporter.

Wait, what – his last year at Liverpool?! Like his teammates Trent and Virgil, Mo's contract was due to run out at the end of the season, but did this mean that he was definitely leaving the club, after eight amazing years? Nooooo, Mo, don't go! The fans were desperate for him to stay longer, and they weren't the only ones.

'They have got to sign Mo Salah up,' said TV pundit

Micah Richards. 'It is imperative they give him a two-year deal.'

After that alarming news, Liverpool lost 1–0 at Anfield against Nottingham Forest, but luckily it turned out to be one single bad day, rather than the start of a bad run. The team got straight back to their winning ways against Bournemouth, with a stunning first-half display:

Luis controlled Ibrahima's long ball and rounded the keeper brilliantly. *1–0!*

Trent dribbled all the way forward from his own half and set up Luis to score his second. *2–0!*

Then, after a one-two with Mo, Darwin cut inside and curled a shot into the far corner. *3–0!*

When the team attacked together with such speed and skill, Slot's stylish new Liverpool side looked absolutely lethal, but could they keep it up all season long? That was the big question. But for now, while his new contract talks carried on in the background, Mo just stayed calm and carried on shining in game after game:

A penalty winner away at Wolves, a chipped cross to Curtis to beat his old club Chelsea, a calm finish on the counterattack to rescue a point against Arsenal. . .

'Come onnnnnnn!' Mo cried out, sliding across the grass on his knees.

Virgil at the back, Ryan in midfield, Luis on the left wing – every single Liverpool player was having an excellent season, but when the team really needed a goalscoring hero, Mo was so often the man who saved the day.

In their next match against Brighton and Hove Albion, the Reds went 1–0 down early in the first half, but they kept attacking and attacking until at last Cody got the equaliser, with 25 minutes to go. Right, now to grab a winner. . .

Less than 90 seconds later, Curtis dribbled forward on the counterattack, played a one-two with Luis, and then set Mo racing away up the right wing.

'Oooooooh!' the Anfield crowd gasped, rising to their feet in anticipation.

Like all defenders, the Brighton left-back knew exactly what Liverpool's Egyptian King wanted to do: cut inside onto his phenomenal left foot. But this time, his touches were so skilful and fast that Pervis Estupiñán couldn't stop him. And once Mo was inside the box, with the space to shoot, there was only one way it was going to end...

Goooooooooooooooooooooooaaaaaaaaaaaaaaaaaaaa aaaaallllllllllllllllllllllllllll!

At first, Mo just stood there in front of the fans with a very serious look on his face, but eventually when Curtis joined the celebrations, he couldn't hold his smile back any longer.

'What a run!' Mo cheered as they high-fived.

'What a finish!' his teammate replied happily.

That winner against Brighton moved Mo up to seven goals and five assists, his best-ever start to a Premier League season. But what mattered most in football was the team, and with ten games played, Liverpool were sitting top of the table, two points above the reigning champions Manchester City.

So, could they keep going and clinch a second Premier League title? Liverpool had a long way to go, but in potentially his last season at the club, Mo was determined to help make it happen.

Pos	Team Name	Played	Wins	Draws	Losses	Goal diff.	Points
1	**Liverpool**	**10**	**8**	**1**	**1**	**13**	**25**
2	Manchester City	10	7	2	1	10	23
3	Nottingham Forest	10	5	4	1	7	19
4	Chelsea	10	5	3	2	8	18
5	Arsenal	10	5	3	2	6	18
6	Aston Villa	10	5	3	2	2	18

PART TWO

ISAK
GAME AFTER GAME,
GOAL AFTER GOAL

After scoring that amazing winner against Arsenal, Alexander was full of confidence again, and when he was feeling good, that's when he always played his best football. So, was he ready to shoot Newcastle back up the Premier League table and into the top six where they belonged?

With his team losing 1–0 at Nottingham Forest, Alexander led their second-half comeback with a quick-reaction finish in the six-yard box, and they went on to win 3–1.

'Yesssssss, that's more like it!' Alexander cheered when the final whistle blew. Newcastle were showing their strong fighting spirit again, they were up to eighth place, and with stars like Sandro Tonali and Harvey Barnes returning to the team, suddenly there were high hopes for the rest of the season.

Those hopes, however, soon faded away after a very disappointing 2–0 defeat at home against West Ham. What, how? Despite dominating the game, Newcastle had paid the price for not taking their chances. Just before half-time, Alexander had found himself one-on-one with the keeper, but after chesting the ball down, he slipped and sliced his shot wide.

'Noooooooooooo!' Alexander groaned and picked himself up off the grass. It was a big chance wasted, but never mind – as a striker, he knew how important it was to move on quickly to the next match and the next goalscoring opportunity. . .

In Newcastle's big game against the league leaders Liverpool, Alexander controlled a brilliant pass from Bruno and skilfully shifted the ball away from Virgil van Dijk and into space. Now what? He was still outside the box, but why not do what he did best? Alexander pulled his right leg back and coolly blasted an unbelievable shot into the top corner. *1–0!*

Goooooooooooooooooooooaaaaaaaaaaaaaaaaaaaa aaaaalllllllllllllllllllllllllll!

What a strike! Racing over to the fans, Alexander pointed back over his shoulder with his thumb, as if to say, 'Did you see what I just did there?' It was a new celebration that he would be using a lot because now that he had started scoring, he just couldn't stop: a header against Brentford, another header against Leicester City. . .

. . . then a first-ever Premier league hat-trick against Ipswich!

Compared with his cracker against Liverpool, all three finishes were pretty scruffy and straightforward, but who cared about that? Alexander certainly didn't as he celebrated in front of the fans with a big smile on his face, and then walked off with the match ball when the final whistle blew. All that really mattered was he was there in the right place at the right time to score, like all the top strikers.

Alexander was now up to ten goals for the season,

but more importantly, Newcastle were back up to eighth place, and only two points behind fifth-placed Bournemouth.

'Come on, we can do this!' Howe urged his players on. It was now looking very likely that the Premier League would be getting FIVE Champions League spots, instead of four, for next season, and so the race was on.

Aston Villa were one of the other teams competing for a top five finish, but when they came to St James' Park, Newcastle cruised to a comfortable 3–0 victory. Anthony scored a screamer within the first two minutes, and then guess who grabbed the second? That's right, Alexander! After some lovely build-up play between Bruno and Jacob Murphy, he burst into the six-yard box to calmly apply the finishing touch.

Goooooooooooooooooooooooaaaaaaaaaaaaaaaaaaaaa aaaaalllllllllllllllllllllllllllll!

No big deal – Alexander was getting used to scoring goal after goal, in game after game. He had now scored at least one in each of his last five Premier League matches in a row! And a week later, away at Manchester United, he made it six.

Playing against a big, strong centre-back like Harry Maguire was never easy, but Alexander was smart and tougher than he looked. Plus, he was on the best form of his life! So, as Lewis Hall delivered a dangerous early cross from the left, Alexander raced in at the back post, closer to United's much smaller centre-back Lisandro Martínez. Then at the last second, he escaped from his marker and *BOOM!* he headed the ball down and past the keeper. *1–0!*

Goooooooooooooooooooooooaaaaaaaaaaaaaaaaaaaa aaaaalllllllllllllllllllllllllllll!

It was Alexander's first-ever goal at the famous Old Trafford, but there was no big celebration, just a few focused fist pumps. Because while Newcastle were ahead, they hadn't won yet.

For the rest of the game, the Manchester United defenders marked Alexander more closely, but he didn't mind because that meant more space for their other attackers. When Anthony curled another teasing ball into the box, Maguire was so busy stopping Newcastle's Number 14 that he didn't spot Joelinton's run until it was too late. *2–0!*

Game won, Newcastle were up to fifth place in the table, and hot on the heels of Chelsea and Nottingham Forest above them too. A top-three Premier League finish – why not? Newcastle were looking solid at the back, powerful in midfield, and up front, they now had one of the best strikers in the world.

But thanks to his latest scoring streak, Alexander had also caught the eye of lots of top European clubs again: Barcelona, Arsenal, PSG, Liverpool. . .

'I don't know if you read the papers, Alexander,' one football reporter asked him after the Manchester United match, 'but there were a few yesterday saying the club had put a £150 million price tag on your head. What's your reaction when you see stories like that?'

'Nooooo, not this again!' Alexander thought to himself, but he answered the question calmly and politely: 'I'm in the middle of the season and I think it's going really well for me and the team, so, you know, all my focus is here and I'm really happy with how things are going. My focus is on the pitch.'

Yes, Alexander had big plans for the second half of the 2024–25 season: winning the EFL Cup, firing Newcastle back into the Champions League, and continuing his great goalscoring form, of course.

SALAH
MAGICIAN ON A MISSION

At the top of the Premier League table, everyone was settling in for another exciting title race between Liverpool and Manchester City, but suddenly, things took a very unexpected turn. In November, Pep Guardiola's reigning champions suffered a spectacular collapse, losing four league games in a row: to Bournemouth, then Brighton, then Tottenham, and then Liverpool!

With City falling apart, the Reds took full advantage at Anfield, and Mo was their star man as usual. Early in the first half, he raced forward to reach Trent's incredible cross-field pass, dribbled into the box, and somehow squeezed an in-perfect cross through the crowded six-yard box, to pick out Cody at the back post. *1–0!*

'Wow, what a ball!' Dominik cheered, racing over to hug Mo first, quickly followed by Cody and Trent.

After that, Virgil and Mo both had great chances to

double Liverpool's lead, but each time, the ball flew just over the bar. Oh dear, would the Reds end up regretting those big misses? No – late in the second half, Luis won a penalty, and up stepped Mo to seal a massive victory for his team. *2–0!*

Goooooooooooooooooooooooaaaaaaaaaaaaaaaaaaaaa aaaaalllllllllllllllllllllllllllll!

Job done – now, how should he celebrate? First, Mo cupped his ear to the roaring crowd, and then he sat down on an advertising board behind the goal and threw his arms in the air. A hero pose – how appropriate!

With only 13 games played, Liverpool were already nine points clear at the top of the Premier League table. With City's downfall, was the title race over before it had even really begun? Not yet – despite two more goals and two more assists from Mo, the Reds could only draw their next two matches against Newcastle and Fulham, and their new title challengers Chelsea managed to close the gap again.

Liverpool were still the league leaders, though. They were playing fast, flowing, attacking football, they had only lost one game all season, and in Mo, they had a magician on a mission. So there was no need to panic. For now, all they had to do was keep calm and keep winning:

Tottenham 3–6 Liverpool

With The Reds running riot, Mo added four more goal contributions to his total: an assist for Dominik, then a tap-in of his own, a simple shot past the keeper. . .

. . . then another assist for Luis. . .

'Come onnnnnnnn!' Mo cried out, punching the air with passion. Hurray, not only were Liverpool bouncing back in style, but he had just become the first player in Premier League history to ever reach double digits in both goals (15) AND assists (10) before Christmas! And there were still two more games to go in 2024. . .

Liverpool 3–1 Leicester

Cody and Curtis got the Reds going on Boxing Day, before Mo finished things off with one of his classic, trademark strikes. From wide on the right wing, he attacked the penalty area at speed, and as the Leicester players backed away, he created just enough space to whip a left-foot shot into the far bottom corner.

Goooooooooooooooooooooooaaaaaaaaaaaaaaaaaaaa aaaaalllllllllllllllllllllllllll!

Every time! Mo made that finish look so easy, but how was he able to keep doing it? There was only one explanation for it: MAGIC! As hard as they tried, there didn't seem to be anything Premier League defenders could do to stop him.

In the title race, Liverpool were looking unstoppable too, but despite their seven-point lead at the top, they were still just taking things one win at a time. . .

West Ham away was supposed to be a tricky trip to London, but instead the Reds totally blew their opponents away. Every time they attacked, they looked like they were going to score. Luis fired in the first, Cody scrambled in the second, and then Mo curled a third past the keeper before half-time.

Goooooooooooooooooooooooaaaaaaaaaaaaaaaaaaaa aaaaalllllllllllllllllllllllllll!

Watching the ball hit the back of the net, Mo didn't even move, but a big smile spread across his face. Why? Because he had just scored his 17th Premier League goal of the season – his 20th in all competitions – and he was simply loving life at Liverpool!

The fun didn't stop there, though. Trent scored a fourth early in the second half, and before the final whistle blew, Diogo made it five, thanks to Mo's 13th Premier League assist of the season so far.

'Mate, you're the best!' Diogo cheered as they hugged and high-fived together.

West Ham 0–5 Liverpool – it was the perfect way for the Reds to say goodbye to 2024, and maintain their strong lead at the top of the table.

Liverpool were still right on track to win their second Premier League title, but what about the other wish at the top of every fan's Christmas list: would their three key players soon be signing new contracts to stay at the club?

'No, we are far away from that,' Mo admitted in an interview after the West Ham win. 'The only thing on my mind is I want Liverpool to win the league and I want to be part of that. I will do my best for the team to win the trophy. There are a few teams catching up with us and we need to stay focused and humble and go again.'

SAKA
A PAINFUL NIGHT AT SELHURST PARK

21 December 2024, Selhurst Park, London

For the second time in four days, Bukayo and his Arsenal teammates were taking on Crystal Palace. In the EFL Cup quarter-finals at the Emirates, the Gunners had won the game 3–2, but could they now do it again in the Premier League, away at Selhurst Park? If they didn't, their title chances could be over before Christmas.

'Come onnnnnn!' Bukayo clapped and cheered as the players were preparing for kick-off.

After the disappointing defeat at Newcastle in early November, Arsenal had bounced back brilliantly to win three games in a row and move to joint-second in the table with Chelsea.

In the first of those three victories, against

Nottingham Forest, Bukayo had been brilliant, scoring the first goal himself after a weaving run, and then setting up the second for Thomas Partey.

Then a week later against West Ham, Bukayo had been even better, grabbing a hat-trick of assists followed by a goal of his own, all before half-time!

'Hurrrrrrraaaaaaaaaaaayyyy!' he yelled out with a beaming smile back on his face.

But since then, Bukayo had struggled in front of goal, along with the rest of Arsenal's attackers. At Fulham, he thought he'd headed home the winner with five minutes to go, but it was ruled out for offside and the match finished 1–1. That had been frustrating enough, but drawing 0–0 at home against Everton was even worse. Despite having 77 per cent of the possession, they'd only managed five shots on target all match.

'Nooooooo!' Bukayo groaned after his volley was well saved by Jordan Pickford. 'Why won't the ball go in today?!'

That poor result had put Arsenal four points behind Chelsea, and seven behind the league leaders Liverpool. So now, against Palace, only a win would do. . .

In the fifth minute of the match, Bukayo got the ball on the right wing and dribbled forward at Chris Richards with intent. The defender refused to let him cut inside onto his favoured left foot, so Bukayo decided to go on the outside, and curl the ball in with his right instead.

He had been working hard on his 'weaker' foot and it showed. Bukayo's cross flew just over Thomas's head, then flicked off Gabriel Magalhães's right leg, and dropped down in front of Gabriel Jesus at the back post. *1–0 to Arsenal!*

'Yesssssss!' Bukayo screamed with joy, racing across the pitch to join the team celebrations. While he wouldn't be getting the official assist, he was pleased with his crucial part in the goal, and the most important thing was that Arsenal were ahead already.

Eight mad minutes later, they were still winning, but 2–1, rather than 1–0. Wow, what an entertaining, end-to-end start to the game! But unfortunately, for Bukayo, his participation in the match was almost done. As he tried to whip another cross into the Palace box, he suddenly felt a sharp pain in the back of his right leg. Owwwwww!

'Uh-oh', Bukayo thought to himself, sitting down on the grass, and shaking his head. 'This isn't good.'

As much as he wanted to carry on playing, he really didn't think that he could, or should, and the Arsenal physio agreed. So, eventually Bukayo limped very slowly off the pitch, and on came Leandro Trossard to take his place.

The Gunners went on to win the match 5–1, but what about Bukayo? How bad was his injury?

'He felt something,' Arteta said straight after the match. 'It is not good news, we have to assess him and wait.'

But two days later, the Arsenal manager gave a more detailed update: 'Unfortunately he will be out for many, many weeks.'

Nooooooooo, what nightmare news, and what terrible timing! Bukayo was going to miss the rest of the busy Christmas period in the Premier League, plus lots of Champions League action too. What were Arsenal going to do without him? In terms of other right-wing options, they only had:

Raheem Sterling, who was also injured, Gabriel Martinelli, who preferred to play on the left...

... and their new wonderkid Ethan Nwaneri, who was still just 17!

But the bigger question for Bukayo was: what was he going to do without Arsenal? At the beginning, he found it hard to deal with the first serious injury of his football career, but after a few days of feeling sorry for himself, he focused on staying true to himself: always strong, always positive, and always smiling.

So, when the surgery on his hamstring went well, he decided to send a social media post straight from his hospital bed. Under a photo of him giving a tired thumbs-up, he wrote a caption: 'The majority see obstacles, but few see the opportunities. Recovery has begun and I'm coming back stronger!'

Back on the football pitch, Arsenal were off to a stuttering but winning start without Bukayo on the wing. Although it wasn't easy or pretty, in the end they managed to beat Ipswich Town 1–0 at the Emirates, thanks to an early goal from Kai.

A quick check of the Premier League table helped to cheer Bukayo up: hurray, Arsenal had moved above Chelsea and into second place!

In their next game on New Year's Day, the Gunners went 1–0 down away at Brentford, but with Bukayo cheering them on from home, they battled back to victory.

First Gabriel Jesus equalised with a diving header. *1–1!*

Then Mikel Merino poked the ball in after a goalmouth scramble. *2–1!*

And finally, Gabriel Martinelli hit a sweet strike into the bottom corner. *3–1!*

Phew, job done, another game won! At the halfway stage of the season, Arsenal were still six points behind the leaders Liverpool, but they weren't giving up on the Premier League title without a fight. And hopefully, they would have their Starboy, Bukayo back to help them sooner, rather than later. . .

Pos	Team Name	Played	Wins	Draws	Losses	Goal diff.	Points
1	**Liverpool**	**18**	**14**	**3**	**1**	**28**	**45**
2	Arsenal	19	11	6	2	21	39
3	Nottingham Forest	19	11	4	4	7	37
4	Chelsea	19	10	5	4	15	35
5	Newcastle	19	9	5	5	11	32
6	Manchester City	19	9	4	6	6	31

PART THREE

SAKA
A LONG SPELL ON THE SIDELINES

Slowly but surely, Bukayo battled his way back to football action. By mid-January, he was ready to return to the Emirates, but only to watch the big derby against Tottenham from the sidelines.

'Welcome back, B!' Declan called out and came over to give him a big hug.

'Hey, be careful with my crutches!' Bukayo replied, but really, it was great to see all of his Arsenal teammates again. Now, could they make sure North London stayed red?

Sure enough, despite going 1–0 down again, the Gunners came back to win, thanks to goals from Gabriel Magalhães and Leandro.

'Get iiiiinnnn!' Bukayo cheered from the stands. How he wished that he could be down there on the pitch celebrating with the others, but no – that fantastic feeling would have to wait a while longer. For now, his team would have to keep fighting on without him. . .

Arsenal 2–2 Aston Villa,
Wolves 0–1 Arsenal,
Arsenal 5–1 Manchester City

Wow, what a victory! It was one of those games where everything just clicked for The Gunners. The whole team pressed together, right from the front, and when the chances came, the players took them brilliantly:

Martin, then Thomas, their defensive midfielder, then left-back Myles Lewis-Skelly, then Kai. . .

. . . and finally, Ethan, with a left-foot curler straight out of the Saka textbook!

While Bukayo was delighted for his super-talented young teammate, he couldn't help thinking, 'Argggh, that should have been *ME* doing that!'

Oh well, seeing the 'new him' shining in an Arsenal shirt was exactly the motivation Bukayo needed to keep going during the long, hard hours of rehab work in the gym. He loved being back at the training ground with his teammates every day, but doing weights and leg exercises on his own was so boring compared to what the others were doing out on the football pitch! Bukayo couldn't wait to be back playing with them again as soon as possible. There was no time to lose; his team needed him!

In the Premier League, Arsenal were still in second place, seven points behind Liverpool, and they had successfully made it through to the Champions League Last 16. But with so many injuries to key players like Bukayo, fighting in four different competitions at the same time had proved impossible.

In January, they were knocked out of the FA Cup on penalties by Manchester United. . .

. . . and then in February, they lost to Newcastle United in the EFL Cup semi-finals.

Noooo – two more opportunities to win trophies wasted! Never mind, at least it did mean the Arsenal squad had some extra time to travel to Dubai for a warm weather training camp, and Bukayo got to go with them. It was so nice to escape the English winter and have some fun in the sun together for a few days, but sadly their time at the camp had a not-so-happy ending: Kai had torn his hamstring, just like Bukayo, and would probably be out for the rest of the season!

With Gabriel Martinelli and Gabriel Jesus also injured, who was going to play in attack for Arsenal? Arghhh – if only they'd signed another striker during the transfer window!

But in more positive news, Bukayo was making good progress, getting closer and closer to his comeback. The Gunners just needed to keep winning for a few more weeks without him. . .

Leicester City 0–2 Arsenal, Arsenal 0–1 West Ham

Noooooo, what a terrible result at West Ham, and the match stats told the story perfectly:

68 per cent possession,

20 shots taken. . .

. . . but only 2 on target!

One goal down, and down to 10-men after Myles's red card, Arsenal created chances to equalise, but they kept falling to the wrong players.

One centre-back, Gabriel Magalhães, blasted a strike over the bar, right-back Ben White fired a fierce shot wide. . .

. . . and then their other centre-back, William Saliba, sent the ball sailing high into the crowd.

'Aaaaaaaaaaah!' Bukayo groaned, watching with growing frustration. It was agony for him, seeing his team struggle like this, and not being able to do anything at all to help them. But day after day on the training pitch, he was pushing himself hard, preparing for his big return. Not long now. . .

Soon, it was game over against West Ham, but was it title race over too? Instead of getting smaller, the gap at the top of the league was widening. Yes, after their win over Manchester City, Liverpool's lead was now up to 11 points! And unfortunately, with the Gunners still missing their best attackers and Mikel Merino playing out of position as a striker, the gap kept growing:

13 points . . .
Nottingham Forest 0–0 Arsenal,
Possession: 63 per cent,
Shots on target: 1

. . . 15 points. . .
Manchester United 1–1 Arsenal,
Possession: 68 per cent,
Shots on target: 6

Overall, it had been a better performance from the Gunners against United, but it was still another two big points dropped. . .

Surely, that was it – the end of their fight to win the Premier League title for another season? But Arteta and his players weren't ready to give up yet, not before March had even begun. Thanks to a clever flick header from Mikel, Arsenal got back to winning ways at home against Chelsea, and the gap was cut down to 12 points again.

'Well done, boys – come on, we can still do this!' Bukayo congratulated his teammates afterwards, buzzing with positivity as always.

Overturning a lead that large by Liverpool, with only nine games to go – it was going to be very, very difficult, but it wasn't impossible. When the Premier League returned in April, after the international break, Arsenal would have their Starboy back at last, after his long, three-month spell on the sidelines. And if anyone could save them from another trophy-less season, then it had to be Bukayo. . .

SALAH
"WE'RE GOING TO WIN THE LEAGUE!"

Back in January 2024, Liverpool had been two points clear at the top of the Premier League table when Mo set off to play for his country Egypt at the Africa Cup of Nations. But a few months and a serious injury later, his team had slipped out of the title race and finished third. So, what were the chances of that happening again?

Well, a year on, in January 2025, the picture looked very different indeed. Liverpool's lead was seven points, they were playing fantastic football, there was no Africa Cup of Nations, and Mo was playing every Premier League game without any sign of injury problems at all. In fact, at the age of 32, he was looking fitter than ever, as well as scoring more goals than ever...

A back-post blast against Ipswich Town, a spot-kick and then a classic curler to beat Bournemouth, another goal and assist in the Merseyside Derby against Everton, the winner against Wolves. . .

. . . and then the opener against Aston Villa.

Goooooooooooooooooooooooaaaaaaaaaaaaaaaaaaaa aaaaaaalllllllllllllllllllllllllllll!

'Come onnnnn!' Mo cheered as he chased after Diogo, who had just set him up with a perfect pass.

Although there was still no sign of a new Liverpool contract, Mo wasn't letting the uncertainty about his future affect his form at all. He had just scored his 24th Premier League goal of the season, in only 26 matches. Wow, it was already his best total since his very first year at the club, in 2017–18, and he still had 12 games to go!

Surely, Mo and his teammates were going to slow down and slip up eventually, though? That's what their main title rivals Arsenal were really hoping, but despite a few more draws, Liverpool had still only lost one Premier League match all season, and that was way back in September! They were now eight points clear at the top, heading into a huge away match against Manchester City.

Since their spectacular collapse back in November, City had got themselves back on the road to recovery, and after making six new signings in the January transfer window, they were now on a run of five league wins out of seven.

Liverpool were definitely in for a tough time at the Etihad, but if they could avoid defeat or even win, then the Premier League title race might be almost over, especially after West Ham's shock victory at Arsenal the previous day.

Ahead of the big game, City's star striker Erling Haaland was ruled out with a knee injury, but Mo, Liverpool's main man in attack, was fighting fit and on fire from the start.

When the Reds won an early corner, they decided to try out a new routine they'd been practising on the training ground. Alexis delivered the ball to the front post, where Luis flicked the ball back towards the penalty spot for Mo, who was unmarked! His first-time shot deflected off a City defender and flew past the keeper. *1–0!*

Goooooooooooooaaaaaaaaaaaaalllllllllllllllllllllll!

'Wow, it worked!' Mo smiled to himself, while his teammates surrounded him and buried him in hugs.

Liverpool were off to a perfect start, and they stayed solid and composed, just like they had all season. A second goal before half-time, however, would put them in an even stronger position...

Mo dropped deep to get the ball and then after playing it back to Trent, he spun and made a bursting run in behind the City defence. The Liverpool right-back picked him out with a beautiful, lofted pass, just like Mo knew he would, leaving him one-on-one with the left-back, Joško Gvardiol.

After taking one touch with his right foot, Mo suddenly twisted and cut inside onto his left, skipping past Gvardiol's outstretched leg. Now, what – shoot? No, there were three City defenders back blocking that option, so instead Mo slipped the ball across to Dominik, who had the time and space to look up and guide a shot into the bottom corner. *2–0!*

'Come onnnnnnn!' Liverpool's goalscorer cried out as he rushed over to Mo, the magician who had created it, and lifted him into the air.

In the second half, Curtis had a third goal ruled out by VAR, but in the end, Mo's two key contributions were enough to win yet another game for his team. All season long, the Egyptian King had been Mr Consistent.

'I can't be bothered talking about him, to be honest!' left-back Andy Robertson joked in an interview after the game, before admitting, 'No, he's been unbelievable.'

That victory over City felt like a very significant moment in Liverpool's season. Because while the title race wasn't technically over yet, the Reds had just beaten the reigning champions for a second time, and they were now 11 points clear at the top. So, it seemed safe for their supporters to start singing in the Manchester rain:

'We're gonna win the league,
We're gonna win the league,
And now you're gonna believe us,
And now you're gonna believe us,
And now you're gonna believe us,

ENGLISH PREMIER LEAGUE

WE'RE GONNA WIN THE LEAGUE!'

The Liverpool players, however, weren't ready to celebrate just yet. They were just going to keep on winning until that precious Premier League trophy was officially in their hands again. . .

Liverpool 2–0 Newcastle
Dominik swept in the first goal, and Alexis smashed in the second, after playing a clever one-two with Mo.
Match won – onto the next one. . .

Liverpool 3–1 Southampton
At half-time, the Reds surprisingly found themselves 1–0 down against the bottom team in the league, but after a triple-substitution to freshen things up, they quickly turned the game around in the second half. Darwin got the equaliser, and then Mo won the match with two powerful penalty kicks, his 26th and 27th Premier League goals of the season.
'Yesssssssssss!' he roared, booting the ball back into

the net in celebration.

Another game, another three points closer to the title – just like Mo's spot-kicks, surely there was no stopping Liverpool now.

ISAK NEWCASTLE'S HISTORY-MAKING HERO

New year, same superstar striker – Alexander's great goalscoring form continued in January 2025: the winner against Tottenham, then two quality finishes to beat Wolves – touch, *BANG!*. . .

Goooooooooooooooooooooooaaaaaaaaaaaaaaaaaaa aaaaaaalllllllllllllllllllllllllllll!

After watching the second one go in, Alexander turned around with his arms out wide, and just soaked up the amazing St James' Park atmosphere.

'Man, you're ridiculous right now!' Bruno cheered, giving him a big hug.

Then to cap off an incredible, all-round performance, Alexander showed that he could do a lot more than just score. Despite being on a hat-trick, he dribbled in off the right wing, faked to go right with a fancy stepover, and instead poked a perfect left-foot pass across to Anthony in space. *3–0!*

'Thanks, mate – that was so unselfish!' Anthony said, as they high-fived and hugged.

For Newcastle, it was their sixth league win in a row, taking them up into the Premier League top four. What a turnaround, considering they'd been down in 12th place in early December!

For Alexander, their superstar striker, it was the eighth league game in a row in which he'd scored at least one goal. He was now only three games off the Premier League record, set by Leicester City's Jamie Vardy during the 2015–16 season. So, could he go on and equal that feat, or even beat it?

Sadly Alexander didn't score at all in Newcastle's next match against Bournemouth, but it didn't mean his fantastic form was over. Just a week later against Southampton, he added two more goals to take his tally up to 17 for the season already! Move over, Haaland – Alexander was now the most lethal striker in the Premier League, and one of the best in the whole world.

He couldn't afford to get carried away, though, and

neither could Newcastle. Chelsea, Manchester City, Aston Villa, Brighton, Bournemouth – these teams were so tightly packed together in the top half of the table, and all it took was two losses for the Magpies to slip back down to seventh, and out of the European spots. Nooooooooo!

A week later, when Nottingham Forest took an early lead at St James' Park, the home fans feared a third defeat in a row, but thankfully, back came Newcastle to win a 4–3 thriller, with Alexander scoring a couple more goals, of course. He was up to 19 goals for the season now, and had already reached a total of 50 in the Premier League! But most importantly, his team had three more points to push them up the table again, and keep their Champions League dream alive.

That wasn't Newcastle's only focus, though – after beating Arsenal in the semis, they were also through to the 2025 EFL Cup final, with the chance to win a major trophy at last, for the first time in 56 years!

So, when their manager Eddie Howe saw that Alexander was struggling with a groin injury, he decided to rest him for their next Premier League game, away against the leaders Liverpool. Without their superstar striker, Newcastle suffered a 2–0 defeat at Anfield, but would the result be different when the two teams met again at Wembley in the EFL Cup final, and with Alexander back in the team and fit again?

Yes! From the kick-off all the way through to the final whistle, Newcastle played with a new level of passion, power, and attacking intent. They were definitely the team on top, but could they turn all their good play into a goal? Just before half-time, Kieran Trippier floated a deep corner towards big Dan Burn on the far side of the box and up he jumped to power a brilliant header into the bottom corner. *1–0!*

'Yessssss!' Watching the ball land in the net, Alexander threw his arms out wide and raced over to join the rest of his team. Newcastle were winning at Wembley!

There was still a long way to go, though – another 45 minutes at least. Could Newcastle really keep up their high-energy gameplan? It seemed they could: early in the second half, another deep corner caused chaos in the Liverpool box. This time, Dan's shot was saved, but the rebound fell to Alexander, and there was no way he was going to miss from three yards. *2–0!*

But no, wait a second – the linesman's flag was up for offside. . .

'No way, I was on!' Alexander protested, waggling his finger in the air, but after a VAR check, it turned out to be Bruno, not him, who had been offside in the build-up.

Oh well – Alexander wasn't going to let one disappointment get him down. Two minutes later, Tino Livramento delivered another dangerous cross into the box, and when Jacob Murphy's header dropped down near the penalty spot, there was Alexander to send the ball swerving into the bottom corner with a swift swipe of his right boot. *2–0!*

Goooooooooooooooooooooooaaaaaaaaaaaaaaaaaaa aaaaaaalllllllllllllllllllllllllllll!

This time, he could celebrate freely, knowing that he had definitely just scored a crucial second for Newcastle in the cup final at Wembley. But while everyone else went wild around him, Alexander still looked as cool and calm as ever. Pointing back over his shoulder with his thumb as usual, he ran over to the corner flag and jumped up high in front of the fans with his arms out wide. What a hero moment, and what a hero feeling!

Eventually, Liverpool did pull one goal back, but it was too little, too late to stop Newcastle from lifting a trophy at last. What a historic moment it was for the club, and who had scored their winner at Wembley? Alexander!

Gimme gimme gimme a striker from Sweden,
He's our Number 14 and he plays in attack.
Gimme gimme gimme a striker from Sweden,
First name's Alexander and his surname's Isak!

Yes, Alexander would be remembered forever as Newcastle's cup-winning hero, but he wasn't stopping there. No, there was still more work to do:

Winning the EFL Cup? *Tick!*

Qualifying for the Champions League? *Not yet!*

As Alexander set off for a busy international break with Sweden, Newcastle sat in sixth place in the

ENGLISH PREMIER LEAGUE

Premier League table, but with a game in hand on the other teams battling for a top-five finish. It was gearing up to be a very tense, exciting end to the season, and Alexander couldn't wait to play his part, scoring more goals to win more games.

Pos	Team Name	Played	Wins	Draws	Losses	Goal diff.	Points
1	**Liverpool**	**29**	**21**	**7**	**1**	**42**	**70**
2	Arsenal	29	16	10	3	29	58
3	Nottingham Forest	29	16	6	7	14	54
4	Chelsea	29	14	7	8	16	49
5	Manchester City	29	14	6	9	15	48
6	Newcastle	28	14	5	9	9	47

SALAH
WINNING THE TITLE
IN STYLE

27 April 2025, Anfield, Liverpool

For months, Liverpool had been running away with the league title, but now at last the day had come when they could officially be crowned champions. If they beat Tottenham at Anfield, then the Reds would win their second Premier League title, and their 20th English league title in total, equalling the record of their great rivals Manchester United.

'Come on, let's do this!' the Liverpool captain Virgil van Dijk said, clapping and cheering as the game kicked off in front of a packed crowd of 60,000 hopeful fans.

So, would Mo be their match-winning hero yet again? After a phenomenal first seven months of the season, his scoring had slowed down a little recently, but with his new, two-year contract finally signed, he was determined to get the job done, and give the supporters something special to celebrate.

Back in early March, the Reds had been on track for a double, maybe even a treble, but in one painful week, they had lost to PSG in the Champions League Last 16 and then to Newcastle in the EFL Cup final. So now, Mo and his teammates were fully focused on winning the one trophy left...

The first goal of the game arrived in the 12th minute, but unfortunately, it was Tottenham, not Liverpool who scored it. When Dominic Solanke's header landed in the net, a stunned silence fell over Anfield. Oh dear – were Spurs about to spoil their Premier League title party?

But the Reds were far too strong, skilful and united to let one goal get them down. Forward they went on the attack straight away, and less than four minutes later, Liverpool were level again. The move started with Mo on the right wing, who poked a perfect pass through to Dominik as he burst into the box, and he then slid the ball across to Luis for a simple tap-in.

Together, they made football look so easy! *1–1!*

Or was it? The assistant referee had raised his flag for offside, but after a long VAR check... the goal was eventually given!

After that, there was no stopping Liverpool on their way to the Premier League title.

Alexis put them in front with a screamer from just outside the penalty area. *2–1!*

And Cody increased their lead before half-time. *3–1!*

Then midway through the second half, Liverpool's main man finally joined in the scoring too. From the right side of the box, Mo cut inside, past the Tottenham left-back, and then instead of curling the ball into the far corner like he often did, he decided to catch the keeper by surprise with a shot at the near post. *BANG!...*

Goooooooooooooooooooooooaaaaaaaaaaaaaaaaaaa aaaaaaalllllllllllllllllllllllllllll!

'Yessssssssssss!' Mo roared, while jumping up and punching the air. Another big game, another great goal! They were so nearly there now...

But before he ran back for the restart, Mo stopped to

share an unforgettable moment with the fans. First, he stood in front of them, proudly tapping the badge on his shirt, then he knelt down to kiss the Anfield grass. Finally, he grabbed a phone and took a celebratory selfie with everyone behind the goal! Their hero was here to stay.

Hurrrraaaaaaaaaaaaayyyyy!

Right, now it was time to get on with the rest of the game...

Six minutes later, Mo almost scored again, but instead, it was Tottenham defender Destiny Udogie who tapped the ball into his own net. *5–1!*

And that was how it ended at Anfield. When the final whistle blew, Mo fell to his knees on the pitch and raised both arms above his head. They had done it; Liverpool had won the league in such style, and with four games to spare. What an achievement, and what a season!

Campeones, Campeones, Olé! Olé! Olé!

Liverpool's only other Premier League title had come back in 2020, during the COVID-19 pandemic, when the players had been forced to celebrate alone in an empty stadium, away from all their supporters. But now, five years later, at a packed Anfield, it was definitely time to get the party started.

Campeones, Campeones, Olé! Olé! Olé!

With a big smile on his face, Mo bounced up and down with all of his amazing teammates. Alisson, Virgil, Trent, Alexis, Dominik, Luis – every single one of them had played a huge part in Liverpool's title success.

'This is what we wanted to deliver to our fans more than anything,' Mo wrote on social media a few days later. 'All teams win games but in the end there's only one champion.'

And there's also only one stand-out superstar! For Mo, there were lots more individual prizes to come during the final weeks of the season: the Golden Boot for finishing as the league's top scorer with 29 goals, the Playmaker award for finishing as the league's top creator with 18 assists, the Football Writers' Association Footballer of the Year. . .

. . . and best of all, the Premier League Player of the Season.

But while Mo was really proud to be the first player to ever win all four awards in the same year, it was the team prizes that would always mean the most to him. He couldn't wait for the final day of the season to arrive, when Liverpool would finally get to lift the Premier League trophy in front of their fans at Anfield.

SAKA
HELLO AGAIN

'Hello again' – that was the two-word message Bukayo posted on social media in late March to announce the news that all Arsenal fans had been waiting for – their Starboy was back!

Although he wasn't ready to play the full 90 minutes of their next Premier League match against Fulham, Bukayo was named on the subs bench, and with 30 minutes to go, Arteta decided it was time to bring him on.

'Arsenal substitution: replacing Number 53 Ethan Nwaneri, Number 7 BUKAYO SAKAAAAAAAA!'

Hurrrraaaaaaaaaaaaaayyyyy!

While the Emirates crowd cheered, Bukayo high-fived Ethan and then ran onto the pitch and straight into the action. Right, where was the ball? He'd missed over three whole months of football – 101 days to be exact – and now he had some catching up to do!

Arsenal were already 1–0 up, but they were going to need another goal to secure the win. . .

While Gabriel Martinelli dribbled forward through the middle, Bukayo stayed wide on the right, but as soon as the Brazilian passed the ball out to Mikel on the left wing, *ZOOM!* Bukayo made his move, bursting into the box at top speed.

When Mikel's cross came in, Gabriel flicked the ball on, and there was Bukayo at the back post, for the easiest of free headers. *2–0!*

Goooooooooooooooooooooooaaaaaaaaaaaaaaaaaa aaaaaaalllllllllllllllllllllllllllll!

'Yesssssssssssss!' It had taken Bukayo just six minutes and 36 seconds to come back with a bang! With a big smile and a cheeky poke of the tongue, he raced over to thank Gabriel and then stood in front of the Arsenal fans making a heart shape with his hands. Man, it felt good to be home again!

BUKAYO! BUKAYO! BUKAYO!

After celebrating with all of his teammates, Bukayo then rushed over to the Arsenal bench. There was one more very special person that he wanted to hug: Sam

Wilson, one of the club's fitness coaches, who had been there with him all the way along his long road to recovery. Bukayo would never forget that, just like he would never forget the night of his beautiful comeback.

But despite the win and his dream return, Arsenal's position in the Premier League didn't change. They were still second, and they were still nine points behind Liverpool, who also had a game in hand. Maybe it was time for the Gunners to switch their main focus to the Champions League instead. . .

For the rest of April, Bukayo continued as a super sub in the Premier League because Arteta was saving him for the big games in Europe:

Arsenal 3–0 Real Madrid

What a win! Declan was the hero of the match with two fantastic free kicks in 12 minutes, but it was Bukayo who won both of them with his deadly dribbling skills.

'We asked and you gave us everything, thank you!' Bukayo wrote to the fans afterwards. 'Same energy in Madrid, job's not finished!'

Real Madrid 1–2 Arsenal

Away at the Bernabéu against Kylian Mbappé, Jude Bellingham and co. Bukayo knew that anything could happen. But if the Gunners could just get one goal, then it might be game over. . .

In the eighth minute, Bukayo had a fierce low shot saved by Thibaut Courtois. . .

. . . and five minutes later, he had a poor 'Panenka'-style penalty saved by the keeper too.

'Noooooooo!' Bukayo groaned with his head in his hands, but he didn't give up. Midway through the second half, he made a smart run from the right wing across the penalty area, before bursting between the Real Madrid centre-backs to reach Mikel's through-ball. . .

Bukayo was one-on-one with Courtois again – could he finally beat the keeper? Yes – as Courtois dived down at his feet, he lifted the ball over him with a clever little chip.

Goooooooooooooooooooooooaaaaaaaaaaaaaaaaaaa aaaaaaalllllllllllllllllllllllllllll!

After cheekily 'Shhh!'-ing the Real Madrid supporters, Bukayo stopped in front of the Arsenal fans and smiled and shrugged. What else did they expect from their beloved Starboy?

This time, Bukayo had an even shorter, one-word message to share on social media: 'Faith'. Bukayo always believed in himself, and in his amazing teammates too. Together, they had just beaten the mighty Real Madrid to reach the Champions League semi-finals!

Arsenal 0–1 PSG

At the Emirates, Bukayo found it tough to beat PSG's excellent left-back Nuno Mendes, but when he swapped wings just before half-time, he almost set up an equaliser for Gabriel Martinelli with a wonderful curling cross. *Oooh, so close!*

PSG 2–1 Arsenal

Away in Paris, Bukayo's first strike was brilliantly tipped over the bar by Gigi Donnarumma, but he did finally score in the 76th minute to make the aggregate score between the two teams 3–1. Game on? Four minutes later, he got another golden chance, but when Riccardo Calafiori's cross bounced in front of him, Bukayo failed to keep calm and blazed his shot high over the bar instead.

'NOOOOOOOOOO!' Bukayo screamed in disbelief. Soon, it was all over and Arsenal were heading out of the Champions League.

Luckily for Bukayo, he didn't have long to dwell on his big miss because back in the Premier League, the Gunners had serious work to do. With only one win in their last five matches, the chasing pack was catching up quickly. Manchester City, Newcastle and Chelsea were all now within four points of second place, and suddenly Arsenal's Champions League spot for next season was under threat.

'Come on, we can't throw this away!' Bukayo told his teammates ahead of their next big match: Liverpool away. By then, the Reds had already been crowned Premier League Champions, but instead of taking it easy, they raced into a two-goal lead.

Uh-oh – Arsenal were in big trouble. They needed

to turn things around quickly, but how? By working together as a team!

Early in the second half, Gabriel Martinelli nodded Leandro's cross down into the bottom corner. *2–1!*

'Let's gooooooo!' Bukayo cried out, throwing his arms up in the air.

Twenty minutes later, he dribbled in off the right wing and set up Martin to hit a thumping strike. The Liverpool keeper managed to push it onto the post, but the ball bounced out to Mikel who scored with a diving header. *2–2!*

After a quick check to make sure the flag wasn't up for offside, Bukayo punched the air with passion. Get in! Arsenal had fought back brilliantly to claim what could be a very precious point. Now, if they could just beat their top-four rivals Newcastle at home at the Emirates, then their Champions League spot would be secured with a game to spare. . .

There were nervy moments in the first half, but some super saves from David Raya kept Arsenal in the game until at last, in the 55th minute, they finally made the breakthrough. The move started with

Bukayo, who won the ball back on the right wing and passed it on to Martin, who fired it across to Declan, who swept an unstoppable shot past the keeper from just outside the box. *1–0!*

'YESSSSSSSSS!' Bukayo cheered as he chased over to Declan.

Forty minutes later, Arsenal were celebrating again. Hurray – they would be playing in the Champions League again next year! But where would they end up in the Premier League table – second, third, or fourth? To find out, they would have to wait until the final day of the season. . .

ISAK CHAMPIONS LEAGUE, HERE WE COME?

Still buzzing from their EFL Cup final triumph, Alexander and his teammates maintained their fine, winning form when the Premier League returned in April.

Newcastle United 2–1 Brentford
Alexander put his team ahead just before half-time, and then Sandro Tonali won the game with a stunning strike.
Job done! Onto the next one...

Leicester City 0–3 Newcastle United
This time, Jacob Murphy was their hero with two goals in the first 11 minutes, and then Harvey Barnes added the third before half-time.
'Yessssssss!' Alexander cheered, raising his arms

in the air. He wasn't the kind of selfish striker who only celebrated when he scored; as long as his team kept winning, then he didn't really care who got the goals. . .

Newcastle United 4–1 Manchester United
Again, Alexander didn't manage to get his name on the scoresheet, but he still played an important part for his team, showing off his skill instead of his shooting. Midway through the first half, he dropped deep to receive the ball from Kieran Trippier, and then flicked it cleverly up and over the top of the defence for Sandro to volley into the net. *1–0!*

'Mate, what a hit!' Alexander cheered happily, and they hugged in front of the fans. As Newcastle's superstar striker, he was used to scoring a lot of the goals himself, but it was great to be sharing the load with his teammates too. . .

Newcastle United 5–0 Crystal Palace
On a wonderful Wednesday night at St James' Park,

the Toon Army simply couldn't stop scoring:

Jacob fired in from a ridiculous angle, Marc Guéhi deflected a cross into his own net, Harvey finished off a quick counterattack, Fabian Schär headed in from a well-worked free kick. . .

. . . and finally, Alexander made it five!

In midfield, Joelinton worked hard to win the ball back, and as it rolled loose, Newcastle's Number 14 was onto it in a flash. From just outside the box, Alexander calmly curled a first-time shot into the bottom corner, like it was the easiest thing in the world.

Goooooooooooooooooooooaaaaaaaaaaaaaaaaaaa aaaaaaalllllllllllllllllllllllllllll!

'There we go!' Alexander told his teammates with a smile. Much better – he'd had enough of missing out on all the scoring fun.

Wow – with five wins in a row, Newcastle were up to third place in the Premier League table, and looking unstoppable! They were now only four points behind second-place Arsenal, with six games still to go. . .

'Champions League, here we come!' their fans

cheered with growing confidence.

Newcastle hadn't qualified for Europe's biggest club competition yet, though; they still had more work to do and more games to win. Alexander scored his 22nd league goal of the season in their successful win over Ipswich Town, and then his 23rd to save the day with a last-minute equaliser away at Brighton.

Gooooooooooooooooooooooaaaaaaaaaaaaaaaaaa aaaaaaalllllllllllllllllllllllllllll!

'Let's gooooooo!' Alexander urged his teammates on as they rushed back for the restart, but unfortunately, it was too late for them to grab a winner.

At the end of a long, hard season, Newcastle's heroes were running out of form and energy at exactly the wrong moment. Following that draw at Brighton, plus disappointing defeats against Aston Villa and Arsenal, they slipped back down the table to fourth place, and suddenly their Champions League chances didn't look so good again:

Oooooooh – what an exciting ending to the season! Five teams were fighting for the last three Champions League places, and they were all separated by just three

Pos	Team Name	Played	Wins	Draws	Losses	Goal diff.	Points
1	**Liverpool (C)**	**37**	**25**	**8**	**4**	**45**	**83**
2	Arsenal	37	19	14	4	34	71
3	Manchester City	37	20	8	9	26	68
4	Newcastle	37	20	6	11	22	66
5	Chelsea	37	19	9	9	20	66
6	Aston Villa	37	19	9	9	9	66
7	Nottingham Forest	37	19	8	10	13	65

points, with only one game to go! Yes, the fight for a top-five Premier League finish was going right down to the final whistle of the final day.

The good news for Newcastle was that their last game would be in front of a loud home crowd at St James' Park, against Everton, a team who were safely in mid-table and hopefully wouldn't have much to play for.

The bad news, though, was that after missing their match against Arsenal due to a groin problem, Alexander was now a major injury doubt for the final day too. Nooooooo, not him, not now!

'He hasn't trained with us yet but he has made good progress through the week,' Howe the manager said in his pre-match press conference. 'There's a chance.'

A chance? Phew, that was better than nothing! Every Newcastle player, coach and fan kept their fingers firmly crossed for Alexander. They really didn't want to go into such an important game without their top-scorer and superstar striker. . .

THE FINAL DAY

25 May 2025, 4:00pm

Liverpool vs Crystal Palace, Anfield
Southampton vs Arsenal, St Mary's Stadium
Newcastle vs Everton, St James' Park

ANFIELD

Although Liverpool had already won the Premier League title, they still wanted to finish the season in style. So, for the last game, their manager Arne Slot named a really strong team, starring Alisson and Virgil van Dijk at the back, and Mo, Luis Díaz and Cody Gakpo in attack.

ST MARY'S STADIUM

With their Champions League spot secured, Arsenal

manager Mikel Arteta decided to make some changes to his team, especially in attack. Ethan Nwaneri and Raheem Sterling both started against Southampton, with Bukayo and Martin Ødegaard dropping down to the subs bench.

ST JAMES' PARK

'. . . and Number 14 Alexander ISAAAAAAAAK!'
Hurrrraaaaaaaaaaaaayyyyy!

Phew, in the end, Newcastle's superstar striker was fit enough to start against Everton. Now, could he fire them to victory and into the Champions League?

9 MINUTES, ANFIELD

The home crowd was hoping for an early goal to celebrate, but instead, it was Crystal Palace who took a shock lead. Collecting the ball on the edge of the box, Ismaïla Sarr had all the time in the world to dribble forward and then slide a shot into the bottom corner. *1–0!*

Oh dear – not the start that Liverpool were looking for, on the day they would be lifting the Premier League trophy...

31 MINUTES, ST JAMES' PARK

With the game still goalless and the tension rising, Newcastle midfielder Sandro Tonali decided to hit a dipping shot from 30 yards out. Jordan Pickford saved it, but he could only push the ball out to the edge of the six-yard box, where Alexander raced forward to reach it first...

Ooooooooooooooooh...

But the angle was tight and his first-time shot flew straight at Pickford. *Double save!*

Ahhhhhhhhhhhhhhh!

Oh well – as things stood, a draw would still be enough to earn Newcastle the top-five finish they wanted...

43 MINUTES, ST MARY'S STADIUM

At last, after a first half full of missed chances, Arsenal finally took the lead at Southampton. Right-back Ben White swung a low cross into the six-yard box, and there, to everyone's surprise, was another defender, Kieran Tierney, to sweep the ball past the keeper. *1–0!*

'Get iiiiiiiiiin!' Bukayo shouted, jumping out of his seat on the subs bench. He was determined to make sure Arsenal finished the season with a win.

56 MINUTES, ST MARY'S STADIUM

Early in the second half, however, Arsenal let their focus slip and Southampton took full advantage, with Ross Stewart heading in the equaliser. *1–1!*

Nooooooooo! On the sidelines, Arteta was furious with his team, and soon it was time for a double substitution:

Leandro Trossard on for Kieran, and Bukayo on

for Raheem.

Hurrrraaaaaaaaaaaaayyyyy!

So, could their Starboy come on and save the day?

65 MINUTES, ST JAMES' PARK

Finally, the ball was in the net, but unfortunately it was bad news for Newcastle. From his position up front, Alexander could only watch in horror as Everton attacker Carlos Alcaraz jumped up and headed a cross down into the bottom corner. *1–0!*

Uh-oh – with Manchester City and Chelsea both winning and Aston Villa drawing, Newcastle had just dropped out of the Champions League places! Alexander and his teammates had some serious work to do now. . .

68 MINUTES, ANFIELD

Despite a few moments of Mo magic, Liverpool were struggling to score against Crystal Palace, and their task got a whole lot harder when defensive midfielder Ryan Gravenberch received a second yellow card and was sent off.

What now? One thing was for sure: even with ten men, Liverpool weren't giving up until the final whistle blew.

73 MINUTES, ST JAMES' PARK

And neither were Newcastle. Kieran Trippier's corner travelled all the way to the back post, where Alexander was waiting, unmarked, to meet it on the volley. *BANG!*

Ooooooooooooooooh...

It was the kind of chance that Alexander usually scored when he was feeling good and fully fit, but not when he was struggling with a groin injury. Instead, sadly he sliced his shot over the bar.

Ahhhhhhhhhhhhhhh!

Five minutes later, however, a loud cheer rang out around St James' Park. Why? Because Aston Villa were losing against Manchester United, which meant Newcastle were back up to fifth place! Could they stay there this time, though?

84 MINUTES, ANFIELD

Were Liverpool heading for only their fifth league defeat of the season? Surely not! With time running out, Darwin Núñez delivered a deep cross to Cody, who headed the ball down for Mo to smash home and save the day yet again. *1–1!*

Gooooooooooooooooooooooaaaaaaaaaaaaaaaaaaa aaaaaaalllllllllllllllllllllllllllll!

'Come onnnnnnnnn!' Mo roared, clenching his fists in front of the fans before grabbing the ball and running back to the halfway line. Because now that Liverpool were finally level, they wanted a winner. . .

ENGLISH PREMIER LEAGUE

89 MINUTES, ST MARY'S STADIUM

At Southampton, Arsenal's attacking pressure finally paid off. With only seconds to go, their captain Martin Ødegaard dribbled across the edge of the box and then fired a swerving shot into the bottom corner. *2–1!*

'Yessssssssssss!' Bukayo cheered, raising both arms in the air. Mission accomplished, at last! Arsenal had ended the Premier League season with a win, and clinched second place for a third year in a row.

95 MINUTES, ST JAMES' PARK

It was all over, and despite a disappointing defeat, Newcastle had done it; they had secured a top-five finish!

Once the great news was officially confirmed, it was time to get the party started at St James' Park. Alexander and his teammates danced around the pitch together as the famous Champions League anthem played.

96 MINUTES, ANFIELD

When the final whistle blew, Liverpool hadn't won the match, but they'd won the Premier League title, and at last it was time for them to lift the precious trophy!

Ohhhhhhhhhhhhhh...

... Hurrrraaaaaaaaaaaaaayyyyy!

Campeones, Campeones, Olé! Olé! Olé!

As the captain, Virgil had the honour of holding the trophy first, but Mo was right behind him on the stage, and his chance soon arrived. After giving the trophy a kiss, he raised it high above his head for all the 60,000 home fans to see. What a feeling, and what a season!

Later on in the title celebrations, the Liverpool players took the crown off the top of the trophy, and guess who they gave it to? Yes – Mo, their incredible Egyptian King.

ENGLISH PREMIER LEAGUE

Pos	Team Name	Played	Wins	Draws	Losses	Goal diff.	Points
1	**Liverpool (C)**	**38**	**25**	**9**	**4**	**45**	**84**
2	Arsenal	38	20	14	4	35	74
3	Manchester City	38	21	8	9	28	71
4	Chelsea	38	20	9	9	21	69
5	Newcastle	38	20	6	12	21	66
6	Aston Villa	38	19	9	10	7	66
7	Nottingham Forest	38	19	8	11	12	65

TOP 5 YOUNG PLAYERS

Few things in football are more exciting than a young player coming from nowhere to take the team by storm. Powered by the spirit of youth, these five took their chance… and ran with it!

AGGIE BEEVER-JONES

Beever-Jones started the season by making her Lionesses debut in a 2–1 friendly win over the Republic of Ireland. She ended it as a domestic treble winner, Chelsea's top goalscorer, and the Women's Football Awards' Young Player of the Season.

Oh, and she also scored her first ever goal for England!

The 2023–24 season may have been her breakthrough, but 2024–25 was when Beever-Jones proved she could mix it with the very best.

'I'm playing with a smile on my face, which is the

main thing,' the Chelsea academy graduate said.

Expect that smile to grow wider: this rising star looks set to keep shining brightly.

 MYLES LEWIS-SKELLY

During Arsenal's bad-tempered 2–2 draw with Manchester City in September 2024, Manchester City's goal-plundering striker Erling Haaland was confronted by Arsenal substitute Lewis-Skelly. 'Who are you?' Haaland scoffed at the 17-year-old. Well, Lewis-Skelly soon made sure that EVERYONE knew who he was.

Later subbed on for his Premier League debut, Lewis-Skelly quickly made Arsenal's left-back position his own – despite being a central midfielder!

Calm, confident and clever, Lewis-Skelly's eye-catching performances were rewarded with a first senior England call-up… and a goal on his international debut!

'To be playing the way he is at just 18 is just ridiculous,' gushed Arsenal and England midfielder Declan Rice.

 DEAN HUIJSEN

Moving to the Premier League against your wishes may seem stressful. But what Bournemouth soon found was that their new centre-back was just a 'Chill Guy'.

Yes, Huijsen arrived from Juventus – for whom he made just one appearance – in the summer of 2024 because the Italian club needed to raise money. Yet the Italian giants were soon kicking themselves…

By December Huijsen was Bournemouth's first-choice centre-back.

By March he'd won his first senior international cap for Spain.

By May he'd been voted as Bournemouth's Player of the Season – no surprise given he made more interceptions, progressive carries and long passes than any other under-21 player in Europe's top five leagues!

In the space of a season Huijsen had quadrupled his value, leading Real Madrid to pay Bournemouth a whopping £50 million for his signature. Your loss, Juventus!

 LAMINE YAMAL

There's a photo taken way back in 2007 of Lamine Yamal, as a baby, being held by a 20-year-old Lionel Messi. Was Yamal being touched by the hands of greatness? Well, with every match that Yamal plays, that photo becomes more of a prophecy. Was Messi choosing the player who would continue his GOAT legacy? Very possibly…

It seems incredible that Lamine Yamal did not turn 18 until July 2025. Seventeen-year-olds are simply not supposed to do the things that Yamal could do. He slalomed through defences, sped through teams, and curled his finishes into top corners (how about those strikes against Inter Milan and Benfica?!).

Without Yamal in the team, who missed several weeks due to injury, Barcelona failed to win any La Liga game. It's been a long time since a player so young has been so important to a team so good…

 DÉSIRÉ DOUÉ

Doué quickly made a name for himself in Paris. He'd impressed at Rennes, with 13 goal contributions in 57 Ligue 1 appearances, leading former teammate Djed Spence to say '[he] is like Neymar reincarnated'.

When it comes to attacking flair, Spence has a point. While some run, Doué glides. With the ball at his feet, he plays with a freedom rarely seen since the Brazilian maestro turned out for PSG.

But when defending, we're not so sure. While Neymar let his teammates do the dirty work, Doué gets stuck in. He made 14 goal contributions in his debut Ligue 1 season with PSG, but saved his best for the Champions League: scoring five, assisting four, and dropping one generational performance in the final.

WOMEN'S SUPER LEAGUE

INTRODUCTION

When the Women's Super League returned in September 2024 for a brand-new season, there was everything to play for. Sure, Chelsea may have won the title for the past five seasons running, but after 12 years, their legendary coach Emma Hayes had left to take charge of the United States Women's National Team. So, were the Blues still favourites under new coach Sonia Bompastor? No one was quite sure.

Chelsea's rivals were queuing up to claim their crown. Last time around, Manchester City had pushed Chelsea all the way, only to lose the title on goal difference on a painful final matchday. Since then, though, City had signed the league's record goalscorer on a free transfer from Arsenal. Would Vivianne Miedema be the player to shoot City to top spot?

Viv's exit had left the Arsenal fans furious. Their title hopes now rested on her replacement, brought in from Barcelona. Might the brilliant Mariona Caldentey transform the Gunners into true trophy contenders?

Manchester United were desperate to play their part in the race for the title, too. While their own new signings looked strong, ace goalkeeper Mary Earps and captain Katie Zelem had both moved abroad, leaving huge boots to fill. Could the Red Devils climb the table without them?

So, would Chelsea win a super sixth WSL title in a row, or would Manchester City, Arsenal, Manchester United or another team altogether knock the champions off their perch? Here's how things unfolded through the eyes of two of the season's brightest stars, Lucy Bronze and Alessia Russo.

CHAPTER 1

LUCY BRONZE
ALL CHANGE AT CHELSEA

Lucy Bronze clicked on the message that flashed up on her phone screen. It was a photo of a pristine changing room at Chelsea's Cobham Training Centre, with the words: Saved you a spot! LJ.

Lucy smiled. It was from her England teammate, Lauren James. The pair had been friends ever since Lauren's very first camp with the Lionesses. Lucy had been happy to help Lauren learn what it meant to become a Lioness… she too had once been that quiet, awkward kid starting out in a team of superstars and knew exactly how Lauren felt. Now it was Lauren's turn to help Lucy settle in to her brand-new club, Chelsea.

Heading inside from Cobham's car park, Lucy felt a

buzz of excitement and nerves, the same feelings she got every time she joined a new club.

It only felt like two minutes since she'd joined Barcelona, where Lucy had added seven trophies to her incredible collection of silverware. Her two seasons in Spain had been sensational, but Lucy had decided it was time to come home to England.

Now she had some new goals. So far, she had won Champions League medals with Barça and Lyon, but never with an English club… that would be something really special. A fourth WSL title was next on her list too. When weighing up who to sign for next there was one clear choice… Lucy felt sure that she could win the most trophies with Chelsea.

It wasn't just Lucy who was beginning a new chapter, the whole club was! At the end of the 2023–24 season, Chelsea had bid a sad farewell to boss Emma Hayes. Emma was easily the best coach in Chelsea's history, leading her side to an incredible seven league titles and five FA Cups. The only trophy that Emma sadly hadn't got her hands on was a big one… the Women's Champions League.

New boss Sonia Bompastor already had two Champions League medals, won as a coach and a player with French club Lyon. Now she was hoping to score a hat-trick with Chelsea.

The trouble was that out of all Chelsea's talented squad, only Cat Macario had a Champions League medal. Sonia would need to make some smart signings, players with experience, passion and a winning mentality. Lucy had all three!

The deal was done in 30 seconds flat, Lucy couldn't wait to team up again with Sonia, her old Lyon boss.

And before they knew it, the first day of pre-season training had rolled around. Captain Millie Bright greeted Lucy with a hearty high-five inside the changing room.

'Welcome to Chelsea!' said Millie. 'We're all buzzing to have you here.'

Millie meant it. She knew from their years together with the Lionesses that Lucy was a born winner and a great leader too. She would make a brilliant Blue!

Sonia's first training session set the standards straightaway. Any player who thought they could slack off, even for a second, risked not being picked for the team. Lucy enjoyed every minute, especially when it came to winning the ball off some of the much younger players.

'Don't you ever slow down?' they gasped.

The answer was no! Lucy had always done everything at a hundred miles an hour, ever since she was a little kid.

By the time the first WSL games arrived, the players felt ready to take on the world. Chelsea began at home against a solid Aston Villa side. Friday night under the lights at Kingsmeadow, what a treat to kick off their season!

A busy first half saw both teams create chances. Lucy came close to scoring a debut goal, only to see her header from a corner well held by Villa goalkeeper Sabrina D'Angelo. Unlucky! Soon after, Chelsea did take the lead. Johanna Rytting Kaneryd's smart curled effort proved a worthy matchwinner in the end. Three points and top spot of the WSL belonged to Chelsea!

As it happened, Lucy grabbed her first Blues goal in the very next game, when Chelsea smashed SEVEN past Crystal Palace. Young striker Aggie Beever-Jones had already put Chelsea one up when Lucy doubled their lead at Selhurst Park.

With Chelsea piling on the pressure, a Palace defender could only half-clear the ball to Lucy, who was bursting into the box. With a single touch, her shot sailed into the top-left corner of the net, cool as you like!

'Get in!' Lucy clenched a fist before her teammates all piled on.

'You see what happens when you hang out with me!' Lauren joked. LJ was the queen of ice-cold finishes!

With an hour gone and Chelsea cruising, Lucy's debut was complete. On came fresh legs to finish the match. After that, the floodgates opened. Lauren tapped home her first goal of the season too, before three more Chelsea stars joined the party: Guro Reiten (twice), Nathalie Björn and Cat Macario.

Final score: Chelsea 7–0 Crystal Palace. What a win! Lucy was living her best life in London!

CHAPTER 2

ALESSIA RUSSO GOAL-SETTING

Across the capital, meanwhile, Alessia Russo was gearing up for her second season at Arsenal. Her first year as a Gunner had gone pretty well – she had been the club's top scorer and they had won the League Cup. But both Alessia and the fans were hungry for more. More good performances, more goals and more trophies. With Viv Miedema no longer an Arsenal player, the pressure was on Alessia's shoulders to keep scoring.

'I'm ready to kick on!' she promised the fans.

Even with Viv gone, there were still plenty of reasons to be positive about the new season. Among Arsenal's new signings were flying forward Mariona

Caldentey, who would wear 'MARIONA' on the back of her shirt and Dutch international keeper Daphne van Domselaar. In pre-season training, the pair slotted into the squad perfectly.

So far, Alessia was loving training alongside Mariona. She could score and assist, creating chances out of thin air. No wonder she was nicknamed 'Super Mario'!

Arsenal's season kicked off with two Champions League qualifiers and two decent wins. Alessia had started both matches, but found herself on the bench for the Gunners' first WSL match, a tricky fixture against rivals Manchester City. Instead, coach Jonas Eidevall chose Stina Blackstenius to lead the line.

Alessia was staying positive, keeping her fingers crossed to get some minutes on the enormous Emirates pitch.

A powerful strike from Frida Maanum soon had Alessia cheering as loudly as the fans, but City drew level before the first half was up. The goalscorer? It had to be... Vivianne Miedema, back to haunt her old club. *Noooooooo!*

The game carried on with Arsenal looking bright.

So when Jess Park's super spin and half-volley put City ahead, just before the hour mark, the Emirates crowd fell into a stunned silence.

Time for action! On came Alessia a few minutes later, in a double substitution with Beth Mead. Could Arsenal's super subs lift the crowd? They would certainly try their best!

With 15 minutes to go, Alessia was put through on goal, but her clipped shot fell too close to City keeper Yamashita to pose any real danger.

'Noooo!' Alessia groaned in frustration. Her finishing was usually much more deadly than that. She jogged back into position, glancing over at Jonas. He stood with his arms folded on the sidelines. Alessia would have to do better than that.

Her next effort had more power, but it still wasn't enough to trouble Yamashita. Jonas stayed silent, while Alessia's shoulders slumped.

Then came the equaliser... Rosa Kafaji was unlucky to see her shot bounce back off the post, but Beth was in the perfect spot to tuck away her shot.

Goooooaaaaalllll!

'Yes, Meado!' Alessia breathed a sigh of relief.

The match ended 2–2. Arsenal had rescued a point, but disappointingly it was two points dropped at home.

A narrow win away to Leicester City came next, followed by a stuttering stalemate with Everton back at the Emirates. Where was the free-flowing football the fans loved to see? Jonas's tactics were stalling, while his players looked short on confidence.

Worse was to come in the Champions League, in a thumping 5–2 defeat at Bayern Munich next. Arsenal were falling apart, with Alessia still stuck on the subs' bench.

Further frustration followed when Arsenal hosted champions Chelsea, in front of another Emirates bumper crowd.

When first-half goals from Chelsea's Mayra Ramírez and Sandy Baltimore put the Blues firmly in control, grumbles began to grow all around the ground. And despite Caitlin Foord pulling a goal back before the break, Chelsea hung on.

Boos blared out at the final whistle. What was happening? Arsenal fans never booed their team!

Alessia could have tried to block it out, but the fans had every right to be upset… Arsenal had looked a shadow of themselves all season.

With emotions running high, tears in the team huddle flooded out. Two points from a possible, the players all knew what that meant… winning the WSL would be almost impossible now, especially with Chelsea looking so unstoppable.

Soon after the defeat, the fans' signs and graffiti demanding 'JONAS OUT' were enough to make Jonas Eidevall quit the club before he was pushed.

Alessia and her teammates were left feeling rocked. Yes, results hadn't been great, but it was sad to see their coach leave in such unhappy circumstances. Alessia would always be thankful to Jonas for bringing her to Arsenal.

The night the news broke, Alessia couldn't sleep. There were too many questions buzzing around her head: *Who will come in next? What style of football will they want to play? Will I keep my place in the team?*

It was close to midnight, but Alessia decided to call

her agent. Luca wouldn't mind, he was also Alessia's brother! And sure enough, he picked up straightaway.

'I know I haven't hit top form yet this season, but the new boss will give me a chance, won't they?' Alessia worried.

'Listen, sis,' Luca advised. 'Just focus on the things that *you* can control… work hard in training, rest, eat well. Forget about everything else. You'll soon find your shooting boots again.' Luca believed in his superstar sister one hundred per cent.

Alessia hung up feeling much more positive. Who knew big brothers could be so wise?

CHAPTER 3

LUCY BRONZE SUPERPOWERED

By the winter break, Chelsea had opened up a six-point gap at the top of the table and were yet to lose a match. Below them, the battle for the other two Champions League places was hotting up, with Man City hit by injuries in second spot and Arsenal scrambling back up the table into third.

Pos	Team Name	Played	Wins	Draws	Losses	Points
1	**Chelsea Women**	**10**	**9**	**1**	**0**	**28**
2	Manchester City Women	10	7	1	2	22
3	Arsenal Women	10	6	3	1	21
4	Manchester Utd Women	37	6	3	1	21
5	Brighton Women	10	5	2	4	17

Chelsea looked invincible, so what did they do? That's right, they made their squad even stronger, bringing in American defender Naomi Girma for a world-record fee, as well as Lucy's long-term teammate at England, Barcelona and Man City, the gifted midfielder Keira Walsh. Both top players, they would add even more quality to Chelsea's talented squad.

The Blues continued their winning ways in January, breezing past Charlton in the FA Cup, before hammering West Ham United away in the WSL.

Then came a big win in a London derby that saw Chelsea remain unbeaten, while Arsenal's own winning run under new boss Renée Slegers came to an end. In a contest that was almost too close to call, substitute Lauren James, back from a long injury, finally proved the difference in the 84th minute.

Lauren was lining up to take a shot when Arsenal skipper Kim Little stuck out a foot that threw the Chelsea player off balance. Penalty! The ref didn't hesitate.

Lucy helped Lauren back to her feet before Guro Reiten stepped up to slot a winning spot-kick past

Daphne van Domselaar. That put Chelsea nine points clear at the top of the WSL. They had one hand on the title already!

And not only were they leading the league, Chelsea were cruising in the cup competitions too, keeping alive their dream of winning all four trophies. An impossible task? Not according to Lucy… it was all she could think about.

Growing up, Lucy always knew she was different. Reading and spelling she found tricky, which her teachers put down to dyslexia. Falling asleep at night was always a struggle too. Then there was football… other kids loved the sport, but Lucy was *obsessed*. She would have trained morning, noon and night if she could have!

It wasn't until she was grown up, just before winning the Euros with England in fact, that Lucy was diagnosed with ADHD and autism. It was a discovery that helped Lucy to understand more about herself. Now she realised why she had always found making eye contact difficult growing up, why she hadn't always loved having hugs and why she had to do everything at one hundred miles an hour. Knowing about her autism didn't change much in Lucy's life, but it did make her realise that she didn't need to try so hard to be like everyone else.

'Lucy's Lucy,' her teammates agreed. Her differences were what made her so special.

In March 2025, Lucy decided to share her story in the news. She wanted to show other people that having autism wasn't something to be hidden away, it was what gave Lucy her hyper focus and her passion for football. 'My autism is my superpower!' she explained proudly.

That same month came a huge test back on the pitch. In a peculiar fixtures pile-up, Chelsea had to play Manchester City four times in a row: in the League Cup final, twice in their Champions League quarter-final, then away in the WSL.

'We're going to be sick of the sight of City!' Lucy joked.

'Bring it on!' said Millie. Chelsea's skipper was always ready to accept the toughest of challenges.

They began with a big one, a trip to Wembley for

Sonia's first final and the chance to win a trophy… the League Cup. City were without Lionesses Lauren Hemp and Alex Greenwood, both sidelined by serious injuries. But in the goal-hungry Bunny Shaw and Vivianne Miedema, they still had plenty of quality.

With the fans swaying and singing in the stands, Mayra Ramírez bundled in from close range to give Chelsea an early lead. 1–0!

City, though, were playing well. Chelsea had to stay switched on.

'If we lose our focus, even for a second, Shaw or Miedema could easily pounce,' Lucy warned her teammates.

But it was another City star, Aoba Fujino, who equalised, letting fly at the end of a mazy run. Hannah Hampton in goal was powerless to stop the shot. Moments later, City almost took the lead, when Mary Fowler robbed Lucy on the edge of her own box. When Fujino slipped the ball to Shaw, the league's top scorer was through one-on-one.

Lucy looked on in horror. 'Come out!' she screamed to Hannah.

Out rushed the Chelsea keeper and made a superb stop with an outstretched boot. *SAVE!*

'Rescued me there!' said Lucy thankfully.

On came Aggie and Maika Hamano to bring a burst of energy. Next, Aggie passed to Mayra on the right wing, who arched a tricky cross into the six-yard box. With Maika about to pounce, City's Hasegawa turned the ball into her own net. *Goooooaaaaalllll!* Sonia's subs were a success straightaway!

Lucy grinned. That was the thing that made this squad winners, whoever left the pitch was replaced by someone just as talented and just as committed.

And win Chelsea did, 2–1, to lift their first silverware of the season.

'One down, three to go!' Lucy clutched the League Cup trophy happily to her chest.

Match No. 2 against City brought Chelsea back down to Earth with a bump. Two Miedema goals from the bench inspired a City win that left Chelsea's Champions League hopes hanging by a thread. Their first defeat of the season stung, but Lucy was staying calm. With a second leg still to play, it wasn't game over just yet.

'We've got players who can score goals for fun,' Lucy told the TV cameras. 'When we're at our best we can beat any team.'

In the teams' third meeting, Chelsea bounced back with a WSL win away at the Etihad. After Kerolin's amazing solo goal had given City the lead, Chelsea could have crumbled. Instead, their gritty second-half performance with goals from Aggie and an injury-time winner from Erin Cuthbert – a brave diving header – sealed three more precious points.

Yessss! Somehow Chelsea always found a way to win. And not only had they taken a huge step closer to retaining the WSL, the victory made everyone believe they could a stage a comeback in the Champions League second leg.

Chelsea's fourth and final match against City was the biggest yet. The Champions League trophy was top of their wish list for Sonia and her players. 2–0 down? Not a problem… Chelsea were ready to win the hard way.

A blistering start in front of the fans at Stamford

Bridge saw Chelsea press high. Lucy led the charge, driving into the box and blasting a shot against the far post. The very next moment though, their other wonderful wing-back thumped home the rebound.

'Baltimore! That's one back!' the commentator roared.

With City struggling, Nathalie Björn headed in Chelsea's second to level the tie next, before Mayra slid in a third goal before the break. 3–0 on the night, Chelsea's Champions League dreams were back on track!

A shell-shocked City never recovered. Chelsea were just too good.

'Come on!' Lucy yelled, as the final whistle blew.

The mighty Barcelona awaited Chelsea in the semi-finals, but Lucy didn't mind.

'Anyone but City!' she and her teammates agreed. Everyone was glad to put their epic four-match battle behind them!

CHAPTER 4

ALESSIA RUSSO RENÉE'S REMARKABLE RUN

While Arsenal began their search for a new manager, their assistant coach Renée Slegers was put in charge of the first team. Only a couple of years older than the Gunners' captain Kim Little, injury had cut short Renée's own playing days. Instead, she had switched to coaching. The players were delighted with the decision! They knew and respected Renée, and with a run of important games ahead of them, were glad she wasn't leaving too.

Training under their new coach was challenging, but something felt different. Renée's tactics weren't quite as strict, she encouraged the Arsenal girls to play with freedom and try to express themselves. Before long, smiles returned to the players' faces that had looked so serious under Jonas.

After training as hard as ever, Alessia waited anxiously for Renée to reveal her first teamsheet. Had Alessia done enough to make the starting 11? Yes, she had! 23 RUSSO, there it was in black and white. Now it was time to repay the coach's trust.

First up was a huge Champions League tie, at home to Swedish champions Vålerenga.

'We know what we have to do,' Renée said in her pre-match team talk. 'The only way to win this is to stick together.'

Alessia nodded. 'We've got this, girls!' she cheered.

A rare goal from defender Emily Fox gave Arsenal and Renée a dream start, scoring with barely 60 seconds on the clock! It was the confidence boost the Gunners needed to go in search of more goals. Caitlin scored next, powering her shot into the roof of the net from a rebound. Soon after, though, the visitors grabbed a goal back.

'We can't switch off like that!' Kim scolded her side. 'No. More. Mistakes.'

Up front Alessia was desperately searching for a third

Arsenal goal, but each shot she unleashed was parried away by the Vålerenga keeper.

'Almost!' Renée encouraged her striker. 'Keep your head up.'

To the new boss, it didn't matter if Alessia missed one, two or even three chances. Renée knew that if her super striker kept believing, eventually one of them would go in.

And one did! With Arsenal now leading 3–1 through Mariona, Alessia latched onto another fine pass from their Spanish star, before rolling a left-foot-finish through the keeper's legs for four! That was one way to impress her new boss! Alessia smiled, feeling a huge weight lift off her shoulders.

'That's my girl!' Leah Williamson congratulated her.

'We've got Lessi Russo – *CLAP, CLAP* – we've got Lessi Russo!' came the chants from the crowd at the final whistle.

Alessia soaked up the Emirates applause, clapping the fans back gratefully.

The Vålerenga result put a welcome stop to Arsenal's poor run of form. Back to business in the WSL next, Arsenal won away at West Ham, then put in a positive performance on the road at Manchester United, with Alessia scoring her first league goal of the season.

'How could you, Less?' United's Ella Toone joked afterwards. It wasn't that long ago that the best friends were lining up together.

Alessia shrugged her shoulders with a twinkle in her eye. *Sorry-not-sorry!*

Then came a huge home win as Arsenal dazzled under the lights back at the Emirates, burying five past an in-form Brighton. And the goals didn't stop there... the Gunners thumped Juventus 4–0 away in the Champions League just days later!

Arsenal's winning run under Renée continued, as the next few matches came thick and fast. All Alessia's efforts on the training pitch were starting to pay off – she shone in every game:

Tottenham Hotspur 0–3 Arsenal, scoring the opening goal in the North London Derby!

Arsenal 1–0 Juventus, almost grabbing an assist!

Arsenal 4–0 Aston Villa, with her first double of the season!

Vålerenga 1–3 Arsenal, bagging another brace!

Liverpool 0–1 Arsenal, scoring the winner!

Arsenal 3–2 Bayern Munich, with a goal and the Player of the Match award!

Wow! Alessia was in red-hot form. She'd scored just once that season with Jonas in charge, but felt fearless under new boss Renée, taking her goals tally to 11 already. What a turnaround!

Arsenal and Alessia headed into the winter break brimming with confidence. Unbeaten in 11 games with Renée at the wheel, ten of those were wins! Suddenly, they found themselves just a point behind second-placed Manchester City in the WSL.

'The Arsenal bosses have to give Renée the job for good, right?' Alessia asked captain Kim.

Not even Kim knew. 'Let's keep everything crossed.'

Whatever happened, there was so much to look forward to in the second half of the season, Arsenal still had four trophies to fight for and the draw for the Champions League quarter-finals wasn't far away. Alessia couldn't wait for a new year to begin.

CHAPTER 5

LUCY BRONZE
THREE CHEERS

Chelsea had made no secret that their Number 1 goal that season was to win the Champions League. Sadly, though, it wasn't to be. Their semi-final saw them suffer two heavy defeats, home and away. Barcelona had been their sensational selves once again, booting Chelsea out of the competition with ease. It felt like a massive opportunity wasted.

The good news was that Sonia felt sure she knew where her tactics had gone wrong. 'We're hurting, but we will learn from this,' the boss told her team. 'We'll come back stronger next season, I promise.'

The players had every reason to believe her – Sonia had led Lyon to Champions League victory once over Barcelona. They felt sure she could do it again with Chelsea.

Everyone's focus switched straight back to the WSL. Arsenal's shock thrashing at Aston Villa meant that Chelsea could wrap up the title even earlier than expected. The Blues only needed a point against Manchester United, but of course had their sights set on taking home all three.

And sure enough, Chelsea found the strength to grind out another victory. Winning was in their DNA! In a match that was end-to-end, it was an experienced player, a leader, who got Chelsea over the line.

With just over a quarter of an hour remaining, Sandy delivered one of her pinpoint corners to be met with a tremendous, towering header from who else? The one and only Lucia Tough Bronze! Millie crushed Lucy in the hugest of bear hugs.

Then at last the whistle blew…

CHELSEA WERE WSL CHAMPIONS FOR THE SIXTH TIME IN A ROW!

The travelling fans went so wild, they made the stand shake!

Champions banners were unfurled and there was dancing in the changing room, but for now the bubbles would have to stay on ice. The WSL may have been done and dusted, but Sonia and her players still had unfinished business.

'Although we've won the league tonight, we want to win our final two games and go unbeaten this season,' Lucy told the TV cameras.

What an achievement that would be! And with the League Cup already in the bank and an FA Cup final still to come, Chelsea remained on course for a treble of trophies!

Three more points at Tottenham Hotspur followed before the final matchday at Stamford Bridge. Being presented with the WSL trophy in front of tens of thousands of home fans was a special way to celebrate winning the league title. Before the game, Chelsea's opponents Liverpool graciously formed a guard of honour, lining up to clap the champions onto the pitch.

With the title already sealed, Chelsea didn't need to win, but the players were determined to end the season in style. Aggie's near-post finish may not have arrived until stoppage time, but it was met with the loudest of cheers from the fans. Aggie was a home-grown hero who had first joined the Blues' academy at the age of nine!

It was a fairy-tale goal that sent records tumbling… Chelsea were champions with a record 60 points and had gone the whole season unbeaten.

'It's official, now we can call ourselves "The Invincibles"!' Lucy said to Aggie.

'Sounds good!' Aggie replied, bursting with pride.

Then at last it was time for the celebrations. Captain Millie raised the blue-ribboned trophy high above her head for all to see, as cameras clicked furiously and golden ticker tape showered the Chelsea squad.

Lucy was on the back row, bouncing on her studs as she waited for her turn to lift the trophy.

Campeones! Campeones! Olé, Olé, Olé! a sea of blue supporters sang.

And even though celebrations like these were nothing new to Lucy (she had more medals than anyone else on the pitch), it felt as thrilling as when she had lifted her very first trophy. Winning never got old!

The party continued with Lucy leading the karaoke in front of the fans and carried on in the changing room. A couple of days later, the monuments of Trafalgar Square even turned blue to honour Chelsea's achievements!

In the end, the celebrations weren't too wild… the players didn't need reminding that they still had one last match of the season to play, the FA Cup final at Wembley Stadium against Manchester United. Win that and not only would they be the Invincibles, they would be treble-winners too!

When Lucy had joined Chelsea at the start of the season, one of her goals was to have a good run in the FA Cup. It was a competition she had fallen in love with at a young age. First, watching some nail-biting men's finals, and years later playing in three women's finals herself. She sometimes had to pinch herself that she got to walk out at Wembley too.

Lucy thought back to her very first FA Cup final, when she had burst onto the scene as a fresh-faced 17-year-old. Her first club, Sunderland, had taken on Arsenal, the queens of the women's game at the time. It had been Lucy's first taste of playing in a big occasion and it had felt incredible. In the end, plucky Sunderland had lost 2–1, but they did themselves proud. Since then, Lucy had won two FA Cup winners' medals with Manchester City and was desperate to make it a hat-trick in Chelsea colours.

Apart from some early Manchester United pressure, the result was never in doubt. The Invincibles turned on the style at Wembley. The opening goal came from a penalty won by Erin and scored by Sandy. A superstar all season long, Sandy powered her penalty past Phallon Tullis-Joyce to give Chelsea a deserved lead on the stroke of half-time.

Super Sandy set up the next goal, too, floating a free-kick towards Cat, who headed home a second for Chelsea late on. United were rocked.

And when Wieke Kaptein pounced on a poor pass-back and chipped the ball across to Sandy in the box, Chelsea's Player of the Match made no mistake in burying her shot into the back of the net. 3–0! What a way to clinch the English treble!

The final whistle was met with enormous cheers and a flurry of flags, waving their appreciation of the players on the Wembley pitch. Soon after, Millie raised Chelsea's third and final trophy of the season, the gleaming FA Cup.

Lucy had almost lost count of the number of medals and cups she'd won over her career. So did she ever get bored of that winning feeling? Absolutely not! She had come to Chelsea to win trophies and had played a huge part in helping the team to win three out of four.

Lucy could be proud of a solid first season back in England. Chelsea were a team with a new coach and new players… they were only going to get better the more they played together. What a terrifying thought for their opponents!

Amid the chaos of the celebrations, Sonia grabbed a quiet word with Lucy. 'So, the Champions League… shall we give it another shot next season?'

'Just try and stop us!' Lucy replied with a beaming smile.

CHAPTER 6

ALESSIA RUSSO
A SENSATIONAL SEASON

Good news greeted the Gunners' players and supporters in January 2025... not only was Renée Slegers staying on as boss after turning around the club's season, but Arsenal had made another exciting signing. Everyone was buzzing when winger Chloe Kelly arrived on loan from rivals Manchester City!

Chloe was low on confidence after being banished to City's bench all season, but was welcomed with open arms at Arsenal. Alessia couldn't wait to link up with her England teammate, Chloe was so good at whipping crosses into the box for strikers to gobble up.

A narrow defeat to Chelsea aside, the Gunners really found their groove in the first few months of the new year, winning nine out of ten games in the WSL. The goals were flying in from all over the pitch. Before long, Alessia was back in the race for the Golden Boot!

And it wasn't just her goals record that Alessia had improved… her hold-up play, physical power and connection with her teammates was stronger than ever. The Arsenal fans couldn't imagine their side without Alessia leading the line.

Having climbed to second place in the table, Arsenal's attentions turned to another competition… the Champions League.

The first leg of their quarter-final ended in defeat, though, with Real Madrid running out 2–0 winners. The Spanish side looked firm favourites to go through to the final four. But by the following week, Renée had everyone believing again. Anything was possible at the Emirates!

'We stay calm and composed,' she instructed. 'We can do this!'

The first half saw Arsenal throw the kitchen sink at the visitors. Chloe sent cross after cross into dangerous areas, but no one could get on the end of any of them.

Anxious faces filled the Emirates stands. On the pitch, though, the players were still full of belief.

As the teams headed back out of the tunnel for the second half, Alessia grabbed a word with Chloe. 'Keep those crosses coming, CK, we'll make one count eventually.'

And sure enough, that's exactly what happened, less than a minute after the restart! When Chloe picked out Alessia at the far post, this time Arsenal's top scorer slid home to give her side lead. Yessss! Now the Gunners were just a goal behind in the tie.

Chloe worked her magic again minutes later, providing a fine assist for Mariona to power home a header, before Alessia added Arsenal's third just before the hour mark. *Goooooooooaaaaalllll!* The Gunners had found top gear!

Now that they had the lead, a determined Arsenal were not about to give it up again.

Nothing was stopping Alessia up front… she found the net twice more in the second half, only for her efforts to be ruled offside by VAR. Gutted!

Everyone was full of emotion at the final whistle.

Arsenal 3–2 Real Madrid on aggregate, Arsenal were unlikely semi-finalists!

Chloe was the first to congratulate Alessia on her Player of the Match performance. 'Well deserved! You were incredible out there.'

'I couldn't have done it without you,' Alessia thanked her.

What a comeback! The reward for all their efforts? A mouth-watering tie against eight-time champions, Lyon.

Lyon showed their experience, edging the first leg 1–2 at the Emirates, with a late winner from Melchie Dumornay. It was a blow, but the Gunners weren't down and out quite yet.

Mariona knew what it took to reach a Champions League final – she already had two winners' medals – and rallied the girls after the defeat. 'It's one goal and it's 90 minutes, so we are alive. We need to keep believing.'

The following week, Arsenal flew to France feeling positive they could pull off another famous comeback.

'It's just one goal, *one single goal*,' Alessia repeated to herself.

Arsenal came flying out from the first whistle,

winning an early corner. Again, Chloe showed her quality, swinging in a set piece that was too hot to handle for Christiane Endler… the ball bounced in off the Lyon keeper's back for an unfortunate own goal. The comeback was on! Next, Mariona found the top corner from 20 yards out. It was a screamer that put Arsenal ahead in the tie 2–1!

Early in the second half, Alessia scored again after another mix-up at the back for Lyon. And when Vanessa Gilles slipped in the box, in stole Caitlin Foord and blasted the ball into the roof of the net. 4–1! This was the stuff of dreams!

A late goal for the hosts did little to dampen the celebrations… with the score now at 5–3, Arsenal were home and dry.

'The Champions League final, how does that feel?' a TV interviewer asked Alessia.

'It gives me goosebumps!' she replied. It meant everything to Arsenal's star striker and her teammates. Not since 2007 had Arsenal reached the final.

After the high of beating Lyon, two terrible results followed in the WSL. First an embarrassing 5–2 loss to strugglers Aston Villa, before another heavy defeat at Brighton. The battle for second place in the league would come down to the last day of the season.

Arsenal v Manchester United. Emirates Stadium. Avoid defeat and Arsenal would finish runners-up to runaway champions Chelsea. Lose again and Manchester United would leapfrog the Gunners and finish second. There was more than just pride on the line.

In a topsy-turvy game, Arsenal let slip a 4–1 lead with the match eventually finishing 4–3. Second place was secured but that made it 12 goals conceded in just three games ... Arsenal would have to seriously tighten up their defence in the Champions League final against Barcelona.

'Attackers like Bonmati and Clàudia Pina will have us on toast!' Kim warned.

The next two weeks were spent resting, training and talking tactics. Barcelona were the best women's team in Europe. To beat them, Arsenal would have to summon up a perfect performance in Lisbon and hope that Barça would be below their brilliant best.

For the first 45, Arsenal didn't put a foot wrong. They even found the back of the net when the ball was turned into her own goal by Irene Paredes. Sadly, VAR judged Frida Maanum offside in the build-up. And even though the goal didn't stand, there it was: the chink in Barcelona's armour that had the Gunners believing.

'We can do this,' Leah said confidently at half time. 'We can really win.'

'Definitely!' a huddle of red shirts agreed.

The minutes ticked on. Barcelona's stars kept on toiling, growing more and more frustrated with every heroic block and tackle that Arsenal's defenders completed.

The Gunners stuck to the game plan, waiting patiently for just one chance to score. Then it came, when Mariona's ball from out wide found substitute Beth on the edge of the D. In a crowded box, Beth slid a brilliantly disguised pass to Stina Blackstenius, who fired through a defender's legs, past keeper Cata Coll and into the far corner.

Goooooooooooaaaaaaaaaaalllllll!

Talk about game-changers, Stina and Beth had only

been on the pitch a matter of minutes! Barcelona were stunned. Could Arsenal hold on to their lead?

Alessia glanced nervously at the stadium clock, showing 90 minutes had passed. Soon after, up went the subs' board. Alessia high-fived defender Lotte Wubben-Moy onto the pitch before joining the other subs, standing shoulder to shoulder on the sideline.

Then, it was all over. Phew! Arsenal had done it, they had made history as CHAMPIONS OF EUROPE!

Hugs, tears and a proud trophy lift followed, as red and white confetti cannoned over the Gunners players and staff. The perfect end to a crazy season.

Even on the flight home to London, it still hadn't sunk in yet. What an unbelievable season... Alessia had scored more goals than ever to share the Golden Boot trophy, she had been voted the Football Writers' Association Women's Footballer of the Year, and now she was a European Champion! Alessia kissed the medal that hung around her neck, gold for a golden girl.

Pos	Team Name	Played	Wins	Draws	Losses	Goal Diff.	Points
1	**Chelsea**	**22**	**19**	**3**	**0**	**43**	**60**
2	Arsenal	22	15	3	4	36	48
3	Manchester United	22	13	5	4	25	44
4	Manchester City	22	13	4	5	21	43
5	Brighton & Hove Albion	22	8	4	10	-6	28
6	Aston Villa	22	7	4	11	-12	25
7	Liverpool	22	7	4	11	-15	25
8	Everton	22	6	6	10	-8	24
9	West Ham United	22	6	5	11	-5	23
10	Leicester City	22	5	5	12	-16	20
11	Tottenham Hotspur	22	5	5	12	-18	20
12	*Crystal Palace*	*22*	*2*	*4*	*16*	*-45*	*10*

WOMEN'S SUPER LEAGUE FINAL TABLE

WOMEN'S SUPER LEAGUE TOP SCORERS

		Goals	Assists	Games
1=	Alessia Russo	12	2	21
1=	Khadija Shaw	12	1	14
3=	Shekiera Martinez	10	0	12
3=	Elisabeth Terland	10	5	20
5=	Viviane Asseyi	9	6	21
5=	Agnes Beever-Jones	9	0	22
5=	Mariona Caldentey	9	5	21
8=	Grace Clinton	8	0	21
8=	Rachel Daly	8	3	22
8=	Bethany England	8	1	19
8=	Guro Reiten	8	0	17

TOP 5 TEAM PERFORMANCES

On some days, everything just clicks. Goalkeepers seem unbeatable, defences solid, midfielders creative and attackers clinical. And when that happens in the most important games, it leads to incredible performances. Just like in these five games...

1. CRYSTAL PALACE 1–0 MANCHESTER CITY, FA CUP FINAL

The odds were stacked against Crystal Palace. In their 119-year history, they had *never* won a major trophy. Now, they faced their greatest test: an FA Cup final against seven-time winners Manchester City.

Still, Crystal Palace fans dared to dream. With attacking talents like Eberechi Eze and Jean-Philippe Mateta, perhaps this could be their year...?

What followed at Wembley was a fantastic defensive display. Palace's players threw their bodies in front of shots and crosses. They charged back and galloped forward. Every tackle seemed to go their way. And even when Manchester City were awarded a penalty, Henderson saved it!

All Palace needed was one attack. Their first of the game was a slick team move that saw full-back Daniel Muñoz cross for starboy Eze to volley home.

The Eagles were soaring… and whatever happened, Manchester City weren't scoring!

'When you always stick together and support each other, you deserve it,' said triumphant manager Oliver Glasner after getting his hands on the FA Cup.

PSG 5–0 INTER MILAN, CHAMPIONS LEAGUE FINAL

It was a game that sent shockwaves around the world. The most dominant display in the history of the Champions League and European Cup. Standout performances from every single PSG player who took to the pitch. Taking home the Champions League trophy at the end of the night? It was the least they deserved.

PSG's players looked like they'd run through brick walls for each other. They were desperate to win the ball in every moment, and once they gained possession, they were able to do what they do best: make magical moments.

Whether it was Dembélé's back heel, Pacho's jaw-dropping tackling, Doué's street skills, Barcola sitting Acerbi down, or Vitinha's ferocious passing and moving, this team gave Inter Milan nightmares.

But the scariest thing for their opponents? This PSG team is one of the youngest in the Champions League. They're only just getting started...

ARSENAL 3–0 REAL MADRID, CHAMPIONS LEAGUE QUARTER-FINAL FIRST LEG

It had been 16 years since Arsenal last went beyond

the quarter-final stage of the Champions League. Standing in their way of a first semi-final since 2009 were 15-time European champions Real Madrid, a team boasting a forward line of Vinicius Jr, Kylian Mbappé and Rodrygo.

Cor… what a test!

The Emirates Stadium was rocking as Arsenal started quickly, energy flowing through their veins. Declan Rice took control from midfield, while Bukayo Saka caused Real Madrid all sorts of problems in attack.

It was Rice who broke the deadlock after 58 minutes as he curled a superb free kick into the corner, cueing wild celebrations. Twelve minutes later, he repeated the trick: another free kick, another goal. There was even time for Mikel Merino to add a third goal with a first-time finish from Myles Lewis-Skelly's pass.

And if it wasn't for goal-line clearances by Jude Bellingham and David Alaba, Arsenal could have won by an even greater margin!

'We had a very complete performance,' purred manager Mikel Arteta.

TOP 5 TEAM PERFORMANCES

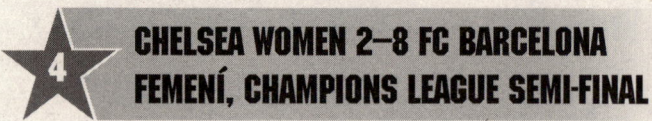

CHELSEA WOMEN 2–8 FC BARCELONA FEMENÍ, CHAMPIONS LEAGUE SEMI-FINAL

This was supposed to be the season that Chelsea Women showed their quality on the greatest stage. Still unbeaten in England, they approached their Champions League semi-final against Barcelona with plenty of hope – only for the reigning European champions to tear them apart over two legs.

Slick, smart and skilful, Barca's brilliant ballers bopped the ball about with ease. Clàudia Pina scored three, Aitana Bonmatí dazzled and Alexia Putellas threatened. If anything, the aggregate scoreline of 2–8 flattered Chelsea: Barcelona could have scored even more!

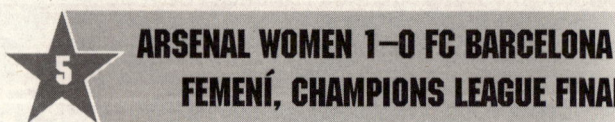

ARSENAL WOMEN 1–0 FC BARCELONA FEMENÍ, CHAMPIONS LEAGUE FINAL

Renée Slegers' side held their very own top team performance competition in this season's Champions

League that saw them christened the 'Comeback Queens'. We could have picked their 3–0 triumph over Real Madrid in the quarter-final, or even their 4–1 semi-final victory over European powerhouses Lyon, but for sheer underdog status we're going with their 1–0 victory over Barcelona in the final.

Going into the game, Arsenal weren't given a chance against a Barcelona side looking to win their third successive Champions League. Even star Barcelona midfielder Aitana Bonmatí admitted she was 'surprised' that Arsenal had made the final.

Yet something incredible happened at the Estádio José Alvalade... this red and white underdog had its day! Arsenal not only kept a clean sheet against Europe's best attack, they also grabbed a goal of their own through Stina Blackstenius, to record a historic win.

WOMEN'S EUROS 2025

WOMEN'S EUROS 2025 REVIEW

When Sarina Wiegman decided to make Hannah Hampton England's new Number 1 ahead of the Euros, the young goalkeeper was buzzing.

'I won't let you down!' Hannah promised the Lionesses boss.

She knew not everyone agreed she was ready to fill the gloves of England legend Mary Earps, but Hannah was ready to prove her doubters wrong. It was something she had been doing her whole life.

Hannah had needed three eye operations by the age of three, and she still struggled to judge how far away objects were. Doctors said Hannah would never play football professionally, yet here she was: England's top keeper!

The tournament in Switzerland would be very different from the last Euros, when England had made history by being crowned European Champions on home soil. Hannah hadn't featured on the pitch at all. This time, she was expected to play every minute.

Thirteen of England's title-winning squad had been chosen again, with Leah Williamson the skipper once more. Sarina had picked some brilliant young Lionesses too!

So, could England make more history and defend their crown?

'We'll give it our best shot!' Hannah told the journalists with a steely gaze.

They would have to dig deep… England had been drawn in a 'Group of Death'.

On a sticky night in Zurich, England kicked off against a dangerous France side. Within 40 seconds, Lauren James fired over… a sure sign that England meant business! And when Alessia Russo struck soon after, the Lionesses fans roared, until VAR ruled the goal offside. Unlucky!

After that, Hannah made a fine save with her boot, but she was helpless to stop Marie-Antoinette Katoto's strike. Just a few minutes later, Sandy Baltimore took advantage of a blunder at the back to put France 2–0 up.

England's second-half subs tried to change the game, but France stood firm. Keira Walsh pulled one back, but it was too late. England were defeated!

Now they had to beat the Netherlands *and* Wales to reach the knockouts. Against Sarina's home nation, though, England were brilliant. Gone were the sloppy passes and the fumbled finishes. England 4, Netherlands 0 – the Lionesses sparkled, and Hannah kept a clean sheet.

Could Wales spoil England's party? No! The Lionesses were 6–1 winners, with six different scorers, and they marched on to the quarter-finals.

'Bring on Sweden!' Hannah cheered. Little did she know what it would take to keep their dream alive!

England were on the back foot straightaway, when Kosovare Asllani struck low into Hannah's far post. And things went from bad to worse when Stina Blackstenius finished off a quick counterattack.

If the England fans thought it was game over, the England squad certainly didn't. Not a single player was ready to go home.

'We're England, we can do this!' Sarina promised, and

made a triple substitution.

The fourth sub Chloe Kelly joined the action next. And within two minutes, she had swung in the perfect assist for Lucy Bronze's goal. At last, England had a lifeline!

The squad's oldest Lioness had scored – now it was over to the youngest! After Sweden failed to clear, teenager Michelle Agyemang slotted home as though she had a hundred caps! Incredible! Just four years earlier, she'd been a Wembley ball girl.

Extra time brought action rather than goals. Leah limped off, then Hannah's nose got bashed, causing a nosebleed. She would have to face penalties with one working nostril!

When Lucy won the coin toss to take the penalties in front of the England fans, it was game on! Alessia put England ahead, but their next THREE penalties were easily saved!

Hannah kept them in it, saving brilliantly from Filippa Angeldahl, while Magdalena Eriksson hit a post. Then Jennifer Falk blazed a spot-kick over the bar, and Chloe coolly converted. To sudden death it went!

'Here we go!' said Hannah, looking ice cold.

Next, she saved from Sofia Jakobsson.

'COME ONNNNNNN!'

Lucy was super cool too. 'If I score this one, then you save the next, we're through,' she told Hannah. It sounded like a plan!

Lucy delivered, almost bursting the net, before Sweden's Smilla Holmberg missed. England had just pulled off the greatest of great escapes to set up a semi-final with Italy!

'Please score some goals this time!' Hannah begged her teammates. Secretly, though, she had loved being the star of the shoot-out and the Player of the Match!

But England went a goal down *again*, after Italy's Barbara Bonansea netted following a lovely flowing move. Nooooooo!

As the clock ticked down, it seemed that the Lionesses' luck was about to run out. On ran Michelle for a nail-biting finish. The next minute, Hannah bravely dived at the feet of Emma Severini to save not once, but twice. Chaos!

England were seconds away from defeat until…

'AGYEMANGGGGGGGGG!' the commentator

screamed. Michelle was England's saviour again!

In extra time, England wore Italy down until they gave away a clumsy penalty… in the very last minute! Chloe did her hop-step-and-strike, but no, it was saved! Thankfully, she gobbled up the rebound.

England 2–1 Italy! Italian tears flowed, while the Lionesses danced in delight.

Was it written in the stars that England and Spain would meet in the final? Some fans thought so. Here was England's chance to put the hurt of the 2023 World Cup final behind them.

It came as no surprise when the world champions scored first. Mariona Caldentey was the villain, heading Spain into the lead. Yet England still believed. All they needed was one chance.

That chance came in the second half, when Chloe 'Clutch' Kelly delivered another perfect cross for Alessia Russo to equalise. 1–1!

Hannah stood tall next, a wall of green, to tip over from Clàudia Pina.

'We're going to win this!' Leah promised Hannah.

Extra time came and went, with some big stars all

subbed off. Hannah wondered who was left to take the penalties!

Beth Mead went first, but slipped and had to take her penalty again. Cata Coll got a glove to it the second time around. Save!

But when Hannah kept out Caldentey and Aitana Bonmatí's strikes next, and Alex Greenwood and Niamh Charles both scored, she felt ten feet tall. Coll saved from Leah, but no matter – Salma Paralluelo shot wide for Spain! If Chloe scored, England would get to keep their trophy!

And of course she did – Chloe's 110-km-an-hour penalty was unstoppable!

'We never give up!' Hannah said proudly.

The Lionesses had done it! They were heroes, every one of the 23, not forgetting their incredible coach, Sarina. Then came the confetti, the choruses of 'Sweet Caroline' and of course the trophy presentation.

England were back-to-back champions, and football was staying home.

TOP 5 INDIVIDUAL PERFORMANCES

Difference-makers. Match-winners. Superstar performers. These five players showed up when it mattered most and took the game by the scruff of its neck. Are these 10 out of 10 performances? We think so...

DAN BURN (NEWCASTLE 2-1 LIVERPOOL, LEAGUE CUP FINAL)

Hometown hero Dan Burn grew up supporting his local team: Newcastle United. He followed them to Wembley in 2000, hoping his team could go on to win their first domestic trophy since 1955. They lost.

Two decades later, he walked onto the Wembley pitch wearing the black-and-white stripes of Newcastle.

It had been a long journey for him, covering release,

rejection, and desperate desire as he worked his way up the Football League pyramid to his boyhood club.

And it had been a long wait for Newcastle. They still hadn't won anything on UK soil for 70 years.

Dan Burn was desperate to change that.

The towering defender had been a colossus all season, and in the week that he received his first England call-up, he put in the performance of a lifetime at Wembley.

He opened the scoring with a thumping header from a corner. He fought for every inch of space, refusing to give Liverpool a sniff. He starved dangerman Mo Salah of any chance to score in a man-of-the-match performance.

But most importantly, his fantastic performance helped Newcastle to a 2–1 win – and their first domestic trophy in 70 years!

 COLE PALMER (CHELSEA 4–2 BRIGHTON, PREMIER LEAGUE)

In Cole Palmer's 2023–24 debut season at Chelsea, he stunned supporters by scoring four goals in a single game as his side beat Everton in a 6–0 win.

TOP 5 INDIVIDUAL PERFORMANCES

In his follow-up season, he went one better…

Seventh-placed Brighton arrived at Stamford Bridge knowing that a win would leapfrog them above Chelsea in the Premier League table. And the game started well for the Seagulls as they took a 1–0 lead.

Step forward Cole Palmer.

First Nicholas Jackson set him up for a pass into an empty net – 1–1!

Then he bagged a penalty – 2–1!

Then a sensational 25-yard free kick – 3–1!

AND THEN an ice-cold finish past Bart Verbruggen… all before half time! 4–2!

Wow, the England international had become the first player in Premier League history to score four goals in the first half of a match.

Surely Cole must have been buzzing after such an incredible performance?!

'I should have had five or six.' Palmer shrugged.

Oh well, maybe next season…

DÉSIRÉ DOUÉ (PSG 5–0 INTER MILAN, CHAMPIONS LEAGUE FINAL)

What do you do if you're 19 years old and playing in your first ever Champions League final? If you're Désiré Doué you simply have fun. His team were magnificent on the night, but Doué was their shining star.

In a supremely confident performance, Doué rouletted, spun full-back Federico Dimarco so much he grew dizzy (and had to be substituted early in the second half), and laid on a composed assist for Achraf Hakimi to open the scoring, before adding two goals of his own.

Three goal involvements in a Champions League final? No player had *ever* done that before.

And Doué had done it all in just 65 minutes, which is when manager Luis Enrique decided to substitute him. Just imagine how much damage the man-of-the-match would have done if he'd played the full 90 minutes...

LEAH WILLIAMSON (ARSENAL 1-0 BARCELONA, CHAMPIONS LEAGUE FINAL)

Stopping Barcelona from scoring? It seemed an impossible task. The Spanish champions' line-up was filled with Ballon d'Or brilliance. And they'd warmed up in the perfect manner, scoring 18 goals across their four knockout matches, during which they blitzed Wolfsburg and Chelsea.

But Barcelona hadn't yet faced Leah Williamson...

Arsenal's defensive dynamo was on top form as she repelled attack after attack. In 90 minutes, she made 14 clearances, two goal-saving blocks and a team-leading 19 defensive actions.

When Arsenal won the Champions League in 2007 Williamson had walked out alongside her heroes as a ten-year-old mascot. Eighteen years later, she was the hero of the night when Arsenal reclaimed their trophy.

5. LAMINE YAMAL (BARCELONA 3–3 INTER MILAN, CHAMPIONS LEAGUE SEMI-FINAL)

One of the best games of the season was lit up by Barcelona's wonderkid. Yamal was relentless, slaloming past defenders with his featherlight footwork. Nobody could stop him – even though he was double, and sometimes triple, marked. He tormented Inter's Federico Dimarco so badly that the full-back had to be subbed off after just 56 minutes. Yamal created for his teammates, and he scored a jaw-dropping opening goal that will live long in the memory, dragging his side back from two goals down to secure an important draw.

'I've never sat in a game and been in so much awe of somebody's performance,' TNT Sports co-commentator Ally McCoist said. 'That was the best 45 minutes I've seen from an individual, maybe anywhere this season.'

Inter Milan boss, Simone Inzaghi, agreed: 'Lamine is the kind of talent that comes along every 50 years.'

EUROPA LEAGUE 2025 REVIEW

'I always win things in my second year. Nothing has changed.'

It was September 2024. Tottenham had just lost to their bitter rivals Arsenal, and Ange Postecoglou was in a fighting mood.

Spurs might have made a sluggish start to the season, but their boss was keen to remind the reporters that his second year as a manager always ended in success.

After all, under Ange's guidance, his teams had all lifted a trophy in year two – whether it was Celtic in Scotland, or Japanese side Yokohama F. Marinos, or in Australia with South Melbourne or Brisbane Roar, or even with its national team.

But in the cutthroat world of English football, could he really repeat the magic with this struggling Spurs team? Especially considering that the north London side hadn't won any silverware since 2007.

While some people raised a disbelieving eyebrow at the manager's prediction, the Spurs players felt inspired by the confidence Ange had in them.

'The boss believes in us, boys,' captain Son Heung-min said to his teammates. 'Ignore what people outside the club are saying. We all know we've got a great squad. Why can't we win a trophy?'

His fellow striker Brennan Johnson nodded: 'Spot on, Sonny. Let's prove the doubters wrong.'

Brennan had been a big-money signing from Nottingham Forest the previous year and loved how the Spurs manager encouraged the team to play a thrilling brand of football. Popularly known as 'Ange-ball', their all-out attacking style delivered plenty of goals – perfect for a hungry striker like Brennan.

However, this season's problem was that the goals were coming at both ends of the pitch and, by February, as Tottenham struggled to find a consistent run of form, their hopes of silverware were looking less likely.

The FA Cup? Knocked out in the fourth round. League Cup? A decent effort but Liverpool ended their spirited run at the semi-final stage. Premier

League? Forget it – Spurs were stuck in the wrong half of the table.

To make matters worse, the squad was ravaged by injuries, with midfield maestro James Maddison and defensive duo Cristian Romero and Micky van de Ven among a long line of players heading to the treatment room.

Tottenham's last chance lay with the Europa League.

'If we're going to end our trophy drought, what better way than winning one of the biggest club competitions in Europe?' Brennan said to Son.

Despite having an injury-stricken squad, Spurs had cruised through the league stage of the competition with five wins and two draws from eight games. Brennan and Sonny led the way with three goals apiece.

Knockout football presents an entirely different challenge, and Spurs raised their game in each round, producing second-leg turnarounds against both AZ Alkmaar and Eintracht Frankfurt. In the first leg of their semi-final, goals from Brennan, Maddison and Dominic Solanke gave them a commanding 3–1 advantage over Norway's Bodø/Glimt.

The return match would be far from easy, however – they had to travel 200km north of the Arctic Circle.

Icy cold conditions? No problem. A plastic pitch? No problem. A comfortable 2–0 win put Spurs into the final.

The trophy dream was very much alive.

Waiting in the final were some familiar opponents – Manchester United. Just like Spurs, United had struggled all season long in the Premier League but had found redemption in the Europa League.

'You can't make it up,' said Brennan. 'You spend the whole competition playing teams from all over Europe and end up in an all-English final.'

'At least we can have a trip to sunny Spain rather than playing them in rainy Manchester again!' Maddison laughed.

Whatever the weather in Bilbao, Spurs had good reason to believe they would do the business. The two sides had already met three times that season, and Tottenham had triumphed each time.

But this would be a very different occasion. Almost 50,000 fans filled the Estadio de San Mamés, a wall of red-and-white shirts at either end of the ground. When the players walked out on to the pitch, they were met with an ear-splitting roar, but all Brennan could hear was the Tottenham fans.

'Oh when the Spurs
Go marching in
Oh when the Spurs go marching in
I want to be in the number
When the Spurs go marching in'

It filled Brennan with pride to know his team had such terrific support. Now it was time to give the fans something to celebrate.

Unsurprisingly, in a high-pressure clash between two teams sitting in the bottom half of the Premier League, the game was far from a classic. Missed passes, stop-start attacks, few chances for either side.

It might not have been the all-attacking style that Spurs were used to, but they gave it everything, digging in, defending solidly and chasing down every ball. And with their talents, they were always going to create a chance – and in the 42nd minute, it arrived.

Finally finding some space on the left wing, Pape

Sarr delivered a dangerous inswinging cross. Brennan was first to react, sneaking in at the near post. He couldn't beat United keeper André Onana but, amid the confusion in the box, the ball bounced off defender Luke Shaw, before – with the tiniest of touches – Brennan poked it into the net.

Goooooaaallllllllll!

For a scrappy game, it was a fittingly messy goal, but none of the Spurs players cared. They were one half of football away from lifting a European trophy.

In the dressing room, Ange reminded his team that the job was far from done.

'For the next 45 minutes,' he told them, 'United will throw everything at us, boys. I want you to defend like you've never defended before.'

Forget 'Ange-ball'. This was 'Ange-wall'. Spurs put 11 players behind the ball and defended as though their lives depended on it. Guglielmo Vicario pulled off a sharp save, Cristian was an immovable rock in the backline, while even Richarlison and Sonny chased back to make crucial blocks.

As the clock was ticking, Guglielmo – coming out for

a cross – could only watch on as a header from Rasmus Højlund soared over him towards the empty net. Then who should appear but Micky, soaring into the air and contorting his body like an acrobat to scoop the ball to safety.

Soon after, Brennan was substituted for defender Kevin Danso while Ange tried to protect the precious lead. Brennan could barely watch from the sidelines as the match entered seven minutes of added time. There was still time for Guglielmo to keep out a header from Shaw, but Spurs would not be denied.

The final whistle blew!

Tottenham were the Europa League champions, Brennan was the matchwinner, and Ange had done it again.

After waiting nearly 20 years to win a trophy, the Spurs fans belted out their famous song long into the Spanish night.

'Glory, glory Tottenham Hotspur
Glory, glory Tottenham Hotspur
Glory, glory Tottenham Hotspur
And the Spurs go marching on!'

Viktoria Plzeň	2		**Bodø/Glimt**	4		Ajax	2		AZ Alkmaar	2
Lazio	3		Olympiacos	2		**Eintracht Frankfurt**	6		**Tottenham Hotspur**	3

Lazio	3 (2)		Eintracht Frankfurt	1
Bodø/Glimt	3 (3)		**Tottenham Hotspur**	2

Tottenham Hotspur	5
Bodø/Glimt	1

Tottenham Hotspur	1
Manchester United	0

Athletic Bilbao	1
Manchester United	7

Rangers	0		Lyon	6
Athletic Bilbao	2		**Manchester United**	7

Rangers	3 (3)		**Athletic Bilbao**	4		FCSB	1		Real Sociedad	2
Fenerbahçe	3 (2)		Roma	3		**Lyon**	7		**Manchester United**	5

EUROPA LEAGUE TOP SCORERS

		Goals	Assists	Games
1=	Bruno Fernandes	7	4	14
1=	Kasper Waarts Høgh	7	1	14
1=	Ayoub El Kaabi	7	0	8
4=	Rasmus Højlund	6	2	15
4=	Václav Černý	6	2	12
4=	Youssef En-Nesyri	6	0	12
4=	Malick Fofana	6	1	10
4=	Samu Aghehowa	6	0	9
4=	Barnabás Varga	6	1	8
4=	Victor Osimhen	6	1	7
11=	Nico Williams	5	2	13
11=	Dominic Solanke	5	4	13
11=	Brennan Johnson	5	1	13
11=	Iñaki Williams	5	1	12

TOP 5 TEAMS

Free-flowing football. Devastating attacks. Dynamic defences. These five teams dominated their opponents, racking up victories and collecting trophies for fun.

1. PSG

What more could this PSG team have achieved?

Champions League: winners

Ligue 1: winners

Trophée des Champions: winners

Coupe de France: winners

That's four trophies out of four, and a first ever quadruple for the French side. But this young team didn't just win… they entertained. Across the season, they scored a ridiculous 152 goals by playing football in a way that was fun and free.

But they also did the dirty work. Every player, from defence to attack, fought for every ball.

'They are a complete side,' said pundit Martin Keown. 'I've never seen forward players working so hard. How do you beat them?'

We, along with the rest of Europe, are still trying to figure that one out, Martin…

BARCELONA

So PSG were fun to watch, but were they the *most* fun team to watch in the world? Barcelona fans would certainly disagree. Their team of superstar attackers plundered 174 goals – more than any other top-level team in Europe! Though their insanely daring high defensive line also meant they conceded a few goals, it only made them even more entertaining.

Hansi Flick's Barcelona side would rather win 5–4 than 1–0, and with a front three of Raphinha, Robert Lewandowski and Yamal, who can blame them?

After suffering in the shadows of Real Madrid for too long, Barca under new boss Flick emerged into the light and stole their rival team's crown. Across the season, they played Real Madrid in four Clásicos – and won all four!

To top it off, Barcelona won a domestic treble of La Liga, Copa del Rey and the Spanish Supercup. They did so by going back to their roots: building the team around La Masia academy graduates like Yamal, Gavi and Cubarsi while playing a beautiful style of football that brought them their most successful season in a decade.

CHELSEA WOMEN

In England they were unstoppable. Invincible. Unbeatable. Yes, Chelsea Women remained unbeaten all season, winning the WSL, the FA Cup AND the League Cup.

No team had ever gone unbeaten in a 22-game WSL season before. And though they crashed out of the Champions League at the semi-final stage, Chelsea's domestic dominance set new standards:

They were the first team to record 60 WSL points.

The first team to twice go unbeaten in a WSL season.

The team with the most ever wins in a WSL season (19).

The first team to win all six of their head-to-head matches against the league's 'big four'.

The first team to win the WSL six times in a row.

And all that despite injured key players like Lauren James, Sam Kerr, Erin Cuthbert and Mayra Ramírez!

FC BARCELONA FEMENÍ

Okay, so Barca didn't win the Champions League. But they won *everything* else. Their team of World Cup winners, Champions League icons, and Ballon d'Or ballers played fantastic football all season. With the intelligence of Aitana Bonmatí, the finishing of Ewa Pajor, and the vision of Alexia Putellas, they recorded some ridiculous results at home and abroad.

Chelsea Women may have gone unbeaten in England, but this Barcelona team stuck eight goals past them over two games. They won their Champions League quarter and semi-finals by a total score of 18–4. They scored 128 goals in Liga F and conceded just 16. They beat Real Madrid 5–0 in the Spanish Super Cup – and they beat Atlético Madrid 2–0 in the Copa de la Reina.

Three out of four trophies ain't bad. But expect this phenomenal Barca team to go all out to regain their cherished Champions League…

LIVERPOOL

Jürgen Klopp was one of Liverpool's greatest managers in the modern era. So when he left after nine seasons in charge, fans may have been concerned. Especially when his replacement, Arne Slot, only brought in one new first team player, Federico Chiesa.

Slot didn't change a great deal on the pitch, either. Using Klopp's tactical foundations, he made a few tweaks: more controlled possession, more passes through the middle, and fewer defensive duties for dangerman Mo Salah.

The changes worked!

Liverpool were rampant as they stormed their way to a 20th Premier League title, finishing ten points ahead of second-placed Arsenal and winning 22 of their first 30 league games.

'It's the best team in the Premier League and the world,' said Brentford manager Thomas Frank, and many agree.

EUROPA CONFERENCE LEAGUE

EUROPA CONFERENCE LEAGUE REVIEW

Chelsea's bid to win the UEFA Conference League almost ended before it had begun.

Facing Servette in a winner-takes-all play-off to get into the main group stage, the Blues were in cruise control, holding a 3–0 lead over the two legs.

Then, out of nowhere, the Swiss side fought back with two goals, wrestling the momentum from their opponents. In the end, only some desperate Chelsea defending and a late Servette miss prevented the tie from going to extra time.

Even Cole Palmer – nicknamed 'Cold Palmer' for his ice-cold personality – was a little flustered.

'You can't take anything for granted in European competition, boys,' he told his teammates. 'Let's not forget this lesson.'

Nine months later, that lesson had definitely been learned by Chelsea. They were on the verge of history, one win away from becoming the first ever team to win all five UEFA club tournaments. After the near-miss against Servette, they won every group game in the Conference League by at least two goals, including an 8–0 thumping of Armenia's FC Noah.

Manager Enzo Maresca had expertly juggled his squad, picking several younger players – all of whom were keen to make an impression – even if that meant they had to go on a 6,000-mile round trip to Kazakhstan.

'I'm happy to sit this one out and give the other lads a chance,' Cole joked with striker Nicolas Jackson ahead of the mammoth journey.

The knockout rounds were a similar story – the Blues swept aside FC Copenhagen, Legia Warsaw and Djurgårdens. In all, they plundered 42 goals in 14 games en route to the final.

A tough test awaited them, however, in the Polish city of Wrocław. Coached by the wily Manuel Pellegrini, who led Manchester City to the 2014 Premier League title, Real Betis had been a revelation in the Conference League, with five-time Champions

League winner Isco pulling the strings in midfield. In the semi-finals, they knocked out Fiorentina who were bidding to reach the final for the third year in a row.

History was on Betis's side, too. Spanish teams – clubs or country – had participated in 27 major finals stretching all the way back to 2002, and had won every single time.

Cole had witnessed it first-hand the previous summer when he was part of the England side that reached the Euro 2024 final. On that occasion, the Three Lions narrowly lost to Spain, despite Cole scoring a superb long-range goal.

Nine minutes into the final in Wrocław, Isco – a player ten years Cole's senior – conjured up the decisive first blow. The veteran midfielder played a sublime pass across the edge of the penalty area to find Abde Ezzalzouli, who fired past Filip Jörgensen.

Cole shared a concerned look with Nicolas. They knew it was going to take something special to stop this Betis side.

For the rest of the half, Chelsea couldn't find the answer, and they had Filip to thank for the score remaining at 1–0, as well as some missed opportunities by their opponents.

Looking at his players as they trudged off the pitch, the manager knew he needed to mix things up if Chelsea were going to get back into the game.

'Reece, get ready! You're going on,' Enzo told club captain Reece James.

Not long after, fellow England internationals Jadon Sancho and Levi Colwill also joined the action, injecting some big-game experience into the line-up.

Yet the Blues still could not find a way past the resolute Betis backline. They needed a moment of magic.

With 25 minutes remaining, Cole found his magician's hat. Drifting down the right wing, he looked up to see Enzo Fernández running into the box.

'On my head, Cole!'

His left-footed cross was inch-perfect, picking out his teammate as he ghosted in between two Betis defenders. Enzo did the rest, guiding his header into the corner of the net.

Betis were rattled, even more so when Cole found

space again, minutes later, on the right wing. With the Spaniards preparing to defend another left-footed inswinger, Cole played the perfect bluff, pulling off a drag-back before sprinting into the box to cross with his right foot. Unlike his opponents, Nicolas was alert to the move and gleefully bundled the ball into the net.

'Not bad with your right foot, mate!' Nicolas laughed while the teammates celebrated their second goal.

In just five minutes, two pieces of wizardry had transformed the final. There might have only been one goal between the teams, but Chelsea had burst the Betis bubble, and their early dominance was now a fast-fading memory.

The team that had barely created a chance in the first half now looked likely to score with every attack.

The game-winning third goal arrived after 83 minutes when another substitute Kiernan Dewsbury-Hall – who featured in all the Conference League matches – found Jadon on the left wing. Jadon's curling shot did the rest.

As the match entered added time, Moisés Caicedo's

strike from the edge of the area completed the comeback and sealed Chelsea's special piece of history.

A few minutes later, while Reece lifted the Conference League trophy into the air, Cole was right in the middle of the celebrations, together with his player of the match award. There were all the usual scenes: confetti, dancing, singing, and spraying of champagne – and when Cole was involved, that was served ice-cold, of course.

JOHN MURRAY

Panathinaikos	4		**Celje**	5 (3)		**Jagiellonia Białystok**	3		**Real Betis**	6
Fiorentina	5		Lugano	5 (1)		Cercle Brugge	2		Vitória de Guimarães	2

Celje	3		**Real Betis**	3
Fiorentina	4		Jagiellonia Białystok	1

Real Betis	4
Fiorentina	3

Real Betis	1
Chelsea	4

Chelsea	5
Djurgårdens IF	1

Rapid Wien	2		**Chelsea**	4
Djurgårdens IF	4		Legia Warsaw	2

Pafos	1		**Rapid Wien**	3		Molde	3		**Chelsea**	3
Djurgårdens IF	3		Borac Banja Luka	2		**Legia Warsaw**	4		Copenhagen	1

	EUROPA CONFERENCE LEAGUE TOP SCORERS			
		Goals	Assists	Games
1	Afimico Pululu	8	8	12
2	Cédric Bakambu	7	2	14
3=	Marc Guiu	6	0	6
3=	Armandas Kučys	6	0	7
4=	Dion Beljo	5	2	10
4=	Johnny Kenny	5	1	6
4=	Rolando Mandragora	5	2	11
4=	Christopher Nkunku	5	3	9
4=	Miloš Pantović	5	1	8
4=	Krzysztof Piątek	5	0	6
5	Abde Ezzalzouli	4	0	13

TOP 5 GOALS

From spectacular strikes to cool conversions, fans were treated to a range of incredible goals. These were five of the best...

AITANA BONMATÍ (CHELSEA 1–4 BARCELONA, CHAMPIONS LEAGUE)

Barcelona's Ballon d'Or holder picked up the ball inside her own half and burst forward, leaving Sjoeke Nüsken in the dust. Sensing danger, Niamh Charles desperately lunged at Bonmatí... but Bonmatí was too quick for her. Byeee!

By now Bonmatí was eating the ground up. As she entered Chelsea's penalty area, Millie Bright moved across from centre-back. Bonmatí's angle was tight, but when Bright threw herself toward the ball she lashed a thumping finish into the roof of the net!

What a goal! And what an important one, too.

Bonmatí's solo strike made it 1–0 to Barcelona on the day – but 5–1 on aggregate. Barcelona's passage to the Champions League final was now secure.

 KAORU MITOMA (BRIGHTON 3–0 CHELSEA, PREMIER LEAGUE)

Mitoma's breathtakingly brilliant goal had a bit of everything. At first glance, it may have appeared that Brighton's keeper Bart Verbruggen had played a hopeful punt upfield… but actually he'd spotted Mitoma's dynamic run between two Chelsea defenders.

Mitoma watched the ball as it sailed over his shoulder from 70 yards, and then stunningly controlled it with a perfectly cushioned touch. His second touch was just as good, moving the ball out of his feet. His third touch pushed him past Chelsea's Trevoh Chalobah before he carefully caressed the ball into the corner of the Chelsea net.

In the space of three seconds, Mitoma had created a magical moment that would live long in the memory. 'The touch is as good as anything we will see in the Premier League this season,' said TV pundit Jamie Carragher.

 OMAR MARMOUSH (MANCHESTER CITY 3–1 BOURNEMOUTH, PREMIER LEAGUE)

It was a game that Manchester City had to win to keep alive their Champions League hopes. And Egyptian forward Marmoush made sure that they won it in style. With the score at 0–0 and 14 minutes gone, he picked up the ball from just inside Bournemouth's half. He looked up, took two touches forward, and then unleashed a dipping piledriver of a shot from 30 yards.

The ball soared past goalkeeper Kepa Arrizabalaga, smashed off the post, and then nestled in the net.

'That's a stunner!' screamed the commentator. 'Nobody was expecting him to score from there.'

4. LAMINE YAMAL (BARCELONA 3–3 INTER MILAN, CHAMPIONS LEAGUE SEMI-FINAL)

Everyone knows what's going to happen: Lamine Yamal will cut inside onto his favourite left foot and curl a shot into the far corner. But can anyone on the pitch stop him from doing it? No way!

It's Yamal's trademark move, and he's done it on the biggest stages and in the biggest moments, including the Champions League semi-final against Inter Milan.

Yamal outmuscled Inter striker Marcus Thuram for possession, then turned toward goal. Running into the area he shimmied to wrongfoot Henrikh Mkhitaryan, took a couple of touches to set himself, then curled a careful strike into the corner. Goalkeeper Yann Sommer didn't even move!

'That moment… in 20 years we'll be sitting and talking about it,' Rio Ferdinand roared on commentary. He wasn't exaggerating – Yamal's goal was later voted as the Champions League's goal of the season!

JAMIE DONLEY (LEYTON ORIENT 1–2 MANCHESTER CITY, FA CUP)

Okay – technically this wasn't actually Jamie Donley's goal. The party poopers at the FA classified it as a Stefan Ortega own goal, but we disagree. Jamie deserves his moment in the spotlight.

With the score at 0–0, Donley raced onto a loose ball just inside the Manchester City half. Most forwards would have taken a touch from so far away, perhaps looking for a pass or to dribble past a defender. Not Jamie Donley. With his first touch he let fly, chipping Ortega from 50 yards!

As his teammates stopped and stared, the ball arced through the air and brushed the crossbar before bouncing in off a hastily retreating Ortega.

What a goal… and what a moment!

Donley was mobbed. Fans threw their limbs all over the place. Little Leyton Orient were 1–0 up against Premier League, Champions League and FA Cup holders Manchester City!

'It's the strike of a lifetime,' said co-commentator

Martin Keown. 'To even think about shooting from there – wow.'

'It is one of the greatest FA Cup goals,' added pundit Chris Sutton.

SERIE A

SERIE A

It was Scott McTominay's fourth league game for Napoli. After just 25 seconds of the game, the Scottish midfielder had sealed a special place in the fans' hearts at his new club.

Scott's first Serie A goal would have been a familiar sight to supporters of Manchester United, the club he had left in the summer for a fresh start in Italy. With Napoli on the attack straight from kick-off against Como, he made a typical surging run from midfield into the box, controlling the ball with his left foot before dispatching it into the far corner with his right.

The goal propelled Napoli to a 3–1 win over Como and marked the start of a beautiful relationship between the club and their new signing.

'Morning Scott... or should I say "McFratm"?' said Billy Gilmour, greeting his teammate at training.

'Uh, morning, pal,' Scott replied with a puzzled frown.

'It's what the Napoli fans are calling you, mate,' Billy

explained. 'The name is a mix of your surname and the Naples word "Fratm", which means "my brother".'

Scott smiled. It was touching to be made to feel so welcome in an unfamiliar city where people spoke a different language, especially after being so used to life at United, where he rose through the ranks from the junior levels all the way to the first team.

It was comforting as well to have Billy by his side. His fellow Scotland international signed for Napoli from Brighton on the same day as Scott. Playing side by side in midfield, the pair formed a central part of Napoli's bid to win a fourth Serie A title.

Their new manager Antonio Conte knew what it took for a team to be champions after he had coached both Juventus and Inter Milan to the Scudetto. He had also guided Chelsea to Premier League glory in 2017.

However, winning another league title would be easier said than done, with some of the best teams in European football standing in their way. Toughest of all was Inter, the defending champions.

In November, the two teams came face to face at the famous San Siro Stadium. Scott got the visitors off to the perfect start, opening the scoring with a clever near-post flick. Just before half-time, Hakan Çalhanoğlu hit back for the home side, who then pressed for a winning goal. Çalhanoğlu had another golden chance when Inter were awarded a penalty but he could only hit the post.

Scott and his teammates breathed a deep sigh of relief.

While the result kept Napoli at the top of the table, Antonio was keen for his players not to get too carried away.

'Great effort today, boys, but remember – there's a long way to go,' he warned. 'Inter are just one point behind us, and so are Atalanta, Fiorentina and Lazio.'

It would take a massive effort to break clear of the chasing pack. With Belgian striker Romelu Lukaku in red-hot form in January, Napoli saw off Fiorentina, Hellas Verona and Atalanta before ending Juventus's 21-game unbeaten run in the league.

But the very next month, they crashed back to earth, only managing three draws from four games.

In such a topsy-turvy season, pretty much the only certainty was Scott's stunning form. He was thriving in a more advanced role up the field, his late runs into the penalty area causing headaches for opposition defences.

On and off the field, Scott was loving life – and one thing, in particular.

'Oh my goodness, the tomatoes! I never ate them at home – they're just red water,' he told reporters. 'Here, they actually taste like tomatoes. Now I eat them as a snack. It's incredible.'

Antonio was happy for Scott to eat as many tomatoes as he liked if he kept tearing up Serie A.

With so little splitting the top teams, the rematch in March between Napoli and Inter Milan shaped up as a crucial encounter. Neither side wanted to hand the advantage to their rivals.

This time, Inter struck the first blow through Federico Dimarco's unstoppable free kick. While time ticked away, the Gli Azzurri found an unlikely hero. With just three minutes remaining, substitute Philip Billing, another Premier League recruit from Bournemouth in the January transfer window, linked up with Stanislav Lobotka.

His first effort was saved, but Philip would not be denied, tapping home the rebound.

'Life in Italy ain't too bad eh, Phil?' Billy said to his new teammate after the final whistle.

'I guess I could get used to this,' Phil replied, looking around at the thousands of cheering fans in the Stadio Diego Armando Maradona.

The points were shared, Napoli and Inter remained inseparable, and so it proved for the rest of the season as the other challengers fell away, leaving the two heavyweights to fight it out for the title.

Champion teams need champion performers, and Scott took his game to an even higher level in April. He scored five goals in three games to earn the Serie A player of the month award and nine vital points for his team.

As Napoli surged, Inter stuttered. A 1–0 loss to Roma handed a slender advantage to the Neopolitans, who clung on to a one-point lead going into the final game. The scenario against Cagliari was simple: if Napoli matched Inter's result at Como, they would be champions.

It quickly became clear they would need to win after an early goal put Inter on their way to a 2–0 victory. When news of the goal reached Naples, the nerves really started to jangle and the home side struggled to find a breakthrough, with Billy denied by a smart save from keeper Alen Sherri.

With half-time approaching, Matteo Politano found a rare bit of space on the right wing.

Scott sensed his chance and surged into the box. 'Matteo, I'm free!' he yelled.

With a defender for close company, that wasn't exactly true, and Matteo's inswinging cross was slightly behind him, but none of that mattered. Scott shrugged off his opponent, then acrobatically volleyed home with his right foot.

Gooooaaaaaalllllll!

'McFratm' had done it again! He had saved his best goal for the most important game of the season.

The goal completely transformed the mood in Naples, both among the players and the fans. Six minutes after half-time, Romelu set off on a bulldozing run, beating two defenders, then the keeper.

The result was in the bag. Napoli had won the Scudetto by a single point. Scott and Billy were the first Scotland internationals to win Serie A since 1905.

And the awards didn't stop there for Scott. In recognition of his 12 goals and six assists, he was named Serie A's Most Valuable Player, the first footballer from Scotland ever to earn the honour.

It was a glorious ending to a remarkable season for the Scotsman who became Naples' favourite son and discovered a new-found love for tomatoes along the way.

SERIE A FINAL TABLE

Pos	Team Name	Played	Wins	Draws	Losses	Goal Diff.	Points
1	**Napoli**	**38**	**24**	**10**	**4**	**32**	**82**
2	Inter	38	24	9	5	44	81
3	Atalanta	38	22	8	8	41	74
4	Juventus	38	18	16	4	23	70
5	Roma	38	20	9	9	21	69
6	Florentina	38	19	8	11	19	65
7	Lazio	38	18	11	9	12	65
8	Milan	38	18	9	11	18	63
9	Bologna	38	16	14	8	10	62
10	Como	38	13	10	15	-3	49
11	Torino	38	10	14	14	-6	44
12	Udinese	38	12	8	18	-15	44
13	Genoa	38	10	13	15	-12	43
14	Verona	38	10	7	21	-32	37
15	Cagliari	38	9	9	20	-16	36
16	Parma	38	7	15	16	-14	36
17	Lecce	38	8	10	20	-31	34
18	*Empoli*	*38*	*6*	*13*	*19*	*-26*	*31*
19	*Venezia*	*38*	*5*	*14*	*19*	*-24*	*29*
20	*Monza*	*38*	*3*	*9*	*26*	*-41*	*18*

SERIE A TOP SCORERS

		Goals	Assists	Games
1	Mateo Retegui	25	8	36
2	Moise Kean	19	3	32
3=	Ademola Lookman	15	5	31
3=	Riccardo Orsolini	15	4	30
5=	Romelu Lukaku	14	10	36
5=	Marcus Thuram	14	4	32
7=	Scott McTominay	12	4	34
7=	Lorenzo Lucca	12	1	33
7=	Arten Dovbyk	12	2	32
7=	Lautaro Martínez	12	3	31

TOP 5 GAMES

End-to-end action! Mistakes! Nutmegs! Worldies! Red cards! Remontadas! Late winners! These five games had it all…

MANCHESTER UNITED 5–4 (7–6) LYON
(EUROPA LEAGUE QUARTER-FINAL SECOND LEG)

With their Premier League season in tatters, all hope for Manchester United rested on success in the Europa League. Having drawn 2–2 in France in the first leg, United were favourites to secure their place in the semi-final.

And as they raced into a 2–0 lead in the second leg, United's players breathed a sigh of relief.

But Lyon had other ideas. Two goals in six second-half minutes saw Lyon level up the tie. Suddenly, United were panicking!

Only for the game to take another twist as Corentin

Tolisso, scorer of Lyon's first goal, was sent off after 89 minutes.

With home advantage and a one-man advantage, the match had swung back in United's favour. Or so the neutrals watching on thought…

Because after 20 minutes of extra time, Lyon had somehow scored two more goals. They were winning 4–2 on the night… and 6–4 on aggregate!

United fans had seen enough. With just ten minutes left, they headed for the exits. 'United need more than a miracle,' observed co-commentator Rio Ferdinand.

But that is exactly what happened…

After 114 minutes Bruno Fernandes made it 4–3.

After 120 minutes, Kobbie Mainoo equalised.

And in injury time of extra-time, centre-back Harry Maguire headed in!

Players, substitutes and staff charged onto the pitch as Maguire wheeled away in celebration. It was the topsy-turvy game that made no sense, 120 minutes of maximum entertainment. And at the end, it was Manchester United who were victorious.

TOP 5 GAMES

BARCELONA 4-3 REAL MADRID (LA LIGA)

There's a reason that a game between Barcelona and Real Madrid is called El Clásico. These games rarely disappoint – and in 2024–25 we were treated to four of them. With 23 goals, four red cards and two trophy wins, we could have chosen any of their clashes for our top 5. But we're going with their fourth, and final, match for the sheer entertainment on offer.

Real Madrid raced into a two-goal lead after 14 minutes, with star forward Kylian Mbappé scoring both. This was a game that they had to win – victory would take them to just one point behind Barcelona in La Liga with three games remaining.

Barcelona, however, knew that they could not afford to lose, and Mbappé's brace woke them up. A hat-trick of Ferran Torres assists later, alongside a Pedri assist, they were back in front. The goals had been scored by Eric García, Yamal and Raphinha (twice)... and the game hadn't even reached half-time!

In the second half, Mbappé completed his hat-trick... but Real Madrid couldn't add a fourth. The game – and the title – was heading to Barcelona.

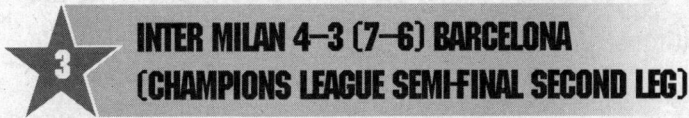 INTER MILAN 4–3 (7–6) BARCELONA (CHAMPIONS LEAGUE SEMI-FINAL SECOND LEG)

The first leg was an instant classic. And the second was even better! With all to play for and the aggregate scoreline at 3–3, both teams pushed hard for glory.

Just like in the first leg, Inter went into a 2–0 lead before half-time. But by the hour mark Barcelona had levelled with goals from Eric García and Dani Olmo – and they were hungry for more. Yamal was unstoppable once again, and when Raphinha smashed home in the 87th minute, it looked like Barcelona would be progressing to the Champions League final.

But this Inter team never gave up. They threw players forward in desperation – including 37-year-old defender Francesco Acerbi, who dramatically provided them with an equaliser in the 93rd minute.

Extra time, then, and this tie was far from over. The game had already had so many twists and turns, and there was time for one more as Davide Frattesi struck home for Inter in the 99th minute.

It was the game that nobody wanted to end – but end it must. At full-time Inter Milan celebrated wildly, while spectators around the world tried to catch their breath!

MANCHESTER CITY 2–2 ARSENAL (PREMIER LEAGUE)

It may only have been September, but this battle was already being billed as a potential title decider: Manchester City, the Premier League holders, against Arsenal, runners-up in each of the last two seasons.

Arsenal hadn't won at the Etihad Stadium since 2015. Could they finally get one over on City?

Though City raced into an early lead through Erling Haaland, Arsenal fought back. A stunning strike from Riccardo Calafiori was followed by a header from Gabriel Magalhães to put Arsenal 2–1 up.

Then, a twist: Arsenal's Leandro Trossard was sent off in first-half injury time for kicking the ball away, and suddenly the game changed.

An angry Arsenal came out for the second half unwilling to let their lead slip. The entire team camped deep inside their half, doing everything to stop City scoring. In response, City pushed their entire team up and let fly shot after shot after shot.

There were 28 second-half shots in total: the joint highest number ever recorded, during a half of Premier League football where Arsenal had just 12.5 per cent possession. It was a half – during a game – that had everything, including a late, late equaliser from John Stones in the 98th minute!

5. MANCHESTER UNITED 2–2 MANCHESTER CITY (WSL)

With Champions League football on the line, there was added spice to this Manchester derby. United needed just a point to qualify for the Champions League, while City had to win to stand any chance of European qualification.

TOP 5 GAMES

Game on!

The Sky Blues started strongly, going 2–0 up inside 42 minutes. But just three minutes later, Grace Clinton had pulled a goal back for United. And midway through the second half, Melvine Malard equalised, to put United within touching distance of Europe.

But their celebrations were short lived. Just one minute after Malard's goal, United substitute Aoife Mannion was sent off for a second bookable offence. United would have to play the last 20 minutes with just ten players!

Old Trafford was rocking while watching United's players throwing themselves in the way of City's attacks. City pushed and pushed, even sending goalkeeper Khiara Keating up to attack in the dying moments. But it was not enough.

United's players jumped for joy at the full-time whistle. They'd survived the drama, written their comeback story, and now they were off to Europe!

SETH BURKETT

BUNDESLIGA

BUNDESLIGA

The player's list of accolades was as impressive as it was long. England's record goalscorer. Three Premier League golden boots. Tottenham Hotspur's top goalscorer. Leading scorer at the World Cup, and at the Euros too. To name just a handful.

Yet for all the awards and the many, many goals, there was one thing missing from Harry Kane's bulging rollcall of honours – he had never won a major trophy with his club or country.

That's not to say he hadn't come close. There had been cup final defeats with Spurs, as well as a runner-up finish in the Premier League, and two incredible runs to the Euros final with England – only to fall just short.

Then there was the previous season in 2023–24, Harry's first with Bayern Munich. The England skipper had arrived in Germany with high hopes. His new team were the kings of German football and had won the previous 11 Bundesliga titles. He quickly settled into his new surroundings, scoring 44 goals in all competitions in his debut season to win the Golden Shoe as the top goalscorer in all of Europe.

Yet, even in such an illustrious first season for Harry at Bayern Munich, he and the rest of the team were denied a trophy in 2024. Their dreams were dashed by surprise package Bayer 04 Leverkusen, who didn't lose a game on their way to the Bundesliga title, winning the German cup for good measure too.

Things like this didn't normally happen to Bayern Munich. So when the next season arrived, Harry – and everyone at the club – only had one thing on their minds. 'The important thing is that we win trophies,' Harry told a room packed full of reporters.

'The question is,' he later said to his teammate Thomas Müller after the TV cameras had left, 'how do we stop the unstoppable Leverkusen?'

'That's easy, my friend,' replied Thomas, a serial winner who had been involved in every one of those 11 Bundesliga triumphs. 'We just keep on winning games.'

'And what's the easiest way to win games? Even

more goals from Harry Kane!' he added, shouting, jumping in the air and pumping his arms, mirroring Harry's famous goalscoring celebration.

Mission set for the new season, Bayern recorded wins over Wolfsburg and Freiburg, then were in merciless mood against Bundesliga newcomers Holstein Kiel. Germany international Jamal Musiala started the onslaught with a goal after just 13 seconds, while former Crystal Palace winger Michael Olise also got on the scoresheet for his new club.

But Harry wasn't going to miss out on the action. By the time he slotted home his third goal – his fifth hat-trick for the club – Bayern had hit their opponents for six and moved to the top of the table.

Their goalfest continued with a 5–0 thrashing of Werder Bremen, with Harry setting another record in the process. His 41st goal made him the Bundesliga's highest English goalscorer, leapfrogging the achievement of Jadon Sancho. 'I'll have to mention that to Jadon next time we meet up for an England game,' Harry chuckled to his teammate and countryman, Eric Dier.

BUNDESLIGA

In fact, the only league game Bayern didn't win in the first two months of the season came against Leverkusen. But crucially, they didn't lose either.

When Robert Andrich put the defending champions ahead midway through the first half, the Bayern players – and most of the anxious fans in the Allianz Arena – could have been forgiven for thinking the pain of the previous season was about to repeat itself. However, this team had a new-found determination and, just eight minutes later, Aleksandar Pavlović's glorious strike from outside the penalty area brought them level.

Points shared. Still top of the league.

Their 100 per cent-winning record may have gone, but Bayern manager Vincent Kompany quickly dispelled any negative feelings. 'Of course, we want to win every game we play, boys, but the main thing today was to show Leverkusen that they can't just turn up and beat us,' Vincent told his players in the dressing room. 'Now they know Bayern Munich is up for the fight.'

Harry knew a thing or two about fights with

Vincent. For many years, the pair had waged some ferocious battles on the field in the Premier League. Tottenham v Manchester City. Star striker v uncompromising defender. Captain v captain.

Now on the same side, their relationship was very different. 'I'm happy for you to score as many goals as you can these days,' Vincent joked.

Three more of those goals from Harry came against Stuttgart in a hat-trick that highlighted the qualities of the Englishman's forward play. The first was a rasping long-range effort into the bottom corner. The second, a cheeky flick over a defender before powering the ball into the net. The third showed his predatory instincts when he reacted quickest to a rebound from close range.

If that wasn't enough, Harry repeated the feat against Augsburg, scoring all three goals in a 3–0 victory, including two fearless penalties.

'I work on penalties a lot. They're a big part of the game,' he revealed in a post-match interview. 'Of course I've missed many at training... but that's the time to miss them!'

BUNDESLIGA

As December dawned, Bayern were full of festive cheer, sitting pretty at the top of the Bundesliga with a seven-point lead. Yet, after 15 seasons in the rollercoaster world of professional football, Harry had learned to take nothing for granted in his quest for a trophy. There was always something unexpected around the corner, and the latest twist came in the shape of a thigh injury that kept him out of the team for three weeks, a period that coincided with the league leaders suffering their first loss of the season at Mainz 04.

Harry cut a frustrated figure on the sidelines.

'I'm desperate to get out there and help the boys,' he said to Thomas.

'Patience, patience, my friend,' his teammate replied calmly. 'We've got a great team of players. What we need is for you to make sure you get fully fit again, so you can help us become even greater.'

Thomas was right, and it wasn't long before Harry was back on the pitch, revelling in a 5–1 thrashing of RB Leipzig that kick-started a run of seven consecutive league wins in which he scored seven goals. When the winning streak eventually came to an end with a goalless draw against – you guessed it! – Leverkusen, Bayern held a comfortable eight-point advantage.

Just as importantly, the destiny of the title was very much in their own hands. And this time, Bayern were not going to let anyone snatch it from their grasp.

Harry's opening goal in a 4–0 demolition of Heidenheim strengthened their grip on the title. This one was extra special as it meant Harry had become the fastest player in the history of the Bundesliga to score 60 goals. It took just 60 games, overtaking previous record-holder Erling Haaland.

But Harry wasn't thinking about individual records. 'All I want is to lift that Bundesliga trophy with you and the boys,' he said to Eric, who had also been part of many of those near-misses with Spurs and England.

Soon, the pain from the end of the 2023–24 season became a far-flung memory. A 3–3 draw at RB Leipzig took Bayern to the brink of the title, and when Leverkusen failed to beat Freiburg the next day, the mission was accomplished.

Bayern were champions!

BUNDESLIGA

While his team celebrated winning the Bundesliga for the 34th time in their history, for Harry it was very much a new feeling – and it couldn't have been any sweeter.

'It's been a long time coming,' he told the media as the celebrations got underway. 'Obviously a lot of hard work, a lot of dedication. It just feels sweet to win the title and the first one of my career.'

And no sooner had the words come out of his mouth, Harry was already starting to think about something else – winning the next one.

JOHN MURRAY

BUNDESLIGA FINAL TABLE

Pos	Team Name	Played	Wins	Draws	Losses	Goal Diff.	Points
1	**Bayern**	34	25	7	2	67	82
2	Leverkusen	34	19	12	3	29	39
3	Eintracht Frankfurt	34	17	9	8	22	60
4	Borussia Dortmund	34	17	6	11	20	57
5	SC Freiburg	34	16	7	11	-4	55
6	1. FSV Mainz 05	34	14	10	10	12	52
7	RB Leipzig	34	13	12	9	5	51
8	SV Werder Bremen	34	14	9	11	-3	51
9	VfB Stuttgart	34	14	8	12	11	50
10	Borussia Mönchengladbach	34	13	6	15	-2	45
11	VfL Wolfsburg	34	11	10	46	2	43
12	FC Augsburg	34	11	10	13	-16	43
13	1. FC Union Berlin	34	10	10	14	-16	40
14	FC St. Pauli	34	8	8	18	-13	32
15	TSG 1899 Hoffenheim	34	7	11	16	-22	32
16	*1. FC Heidenheim*	*34*	*8*	*5*	*21*	*-27*	*29*
17	*Holstein Kiel*	*34*	*6*	*7*	*21*	*-31*	*25*
18	*VfL Bochum 1848*	*34*	*6*	*7*	*21*	*-31*	*25*

BUNDESLIGA TOP SCORERS				
		Goals	Assists	Games
1	Harry Kane	26	10	31
2=	Patrick Schick	21	1	31
2=	Serhou Guirassy	21	4	30
4	Jonathan Burkardt	18	3	29
5	Tim Kleindienst	16	9	31
6=	Omar Marmoush	15	10	17
6=	Hugo Ekitiké	15	8	33
6=	Ermedin Demirović	15	2	34
9	Benjamin Šeško	13	5	33
10	Nick Woltemade	12	2	28

TOP 5 SIGNINGS

For every transfer window, fans demand that their clubs spend mega-money to recruit their next superstars! The fee was definitely worth it for these five players…

SCOTT MCTOMINAY (MANCHESTER UNITED TO NAPOLI, £25.7M)

It's easy to see why former Manchester United manager Erik ten Hag didn't want to sell Scott McTominay. In his debut season in Italy, McTominay was named as Serie A's MVP (Most Valuable Player), scored 12 goals, made six assists, won the Serie A league title, and became a Napoli icon.

Operating as an attacking midfielder, McTominay proved himself to be tough tackling (his 208 duels won was the second highest individual number in the whole league), a clutch goal scorer (eight of his 12 goals came with the score at 0–0), and a devastating partner to striker Romelu Lukaku.

The fans christened him 'McFratm', which roughly translates as 'McBro'. They sang songs about him, wore kilts to games, inked tattoos of him, and even created a shrine in his honour.

KHVICHA KVARATSKHELIA (NAPOLI TO PSG, £59M)

PSG, the most dominant champions in Champions League history, *almost* didn't make it out of the group stages. With six games played, the French champions sat in 25th position – one place out of the play-off positions and nine places below automatic qualifications. They had just two games to change their fortunes. So what did they do?

They signed Kvaratskhelia.

The maverick midfielder with the hard-to-spell name slotted in on the left and instantly showed his talent. He dribbled at defenders, scored and created, but most importantly for manager Luis Enrique, he worked hard for his team.

He may not have been allowed to play until the play-off stage of the Champions League, but once he got his chance, he took it with both feet. In the nine European games 'Kvaradona' played, PSG scored a total of 24 goals. But more than that: they turned on the style.

Much of that was down to their star Georgian signing, who finished a fantastic season with Ligue 1, Serie A, French Cup and Champions League winners' medals – not a bad haul!

MATZ SELS (STRASBOURG TO NOTTINGHAM FOREST, £5.1M)

Signing a goalkeeper who'd been a second-choice Championship keeper didn't exactly set Nottingham Forest's fans' hearts racing. Plenty of them hadn't even heard of Matz Sels, who'd made just nine appearances for Newcastle during a brief spell in the second tier of English football.

Not even good enough for the Championship? Surely he couldn't make the step up to the Premier League from his latest club, Strasbourg. Could he?

Sels had one simple word for those doubters: yes.

Across the Premier League season, he had made 120 saves. Only three goalkeepers made more!

In fact, Sels saved 72.1 per cent of the shots he faced. That's the second highest figure in the Premier League!

In March 2025, he won the Premier League's Save of the Month award with an incredible stop against Liverpool.

And in May, Sels shared the Premier League's Golden Glove award with Arsenal's David Raya after keeping a league-leading 13 clean sheets – nine more than Forest managed the previous season!

Sels' heroics catapulted Forest from relegation favourites to European qualification – what a signing.

MARIONA CALDENTEY (BARCELONA TO ARSENAL, FREE TRANSFER)

She had won 25 trophies in 10 years at Barcelona – and a World Cup for Spain. Arsenal's recruitment team had identified her as one of the best players in the world who could take the club to the next level. They had to sign her!

And at the end of her Barcelona contract, they did just that.

Within days of arriving in North London, Caldentey proved her class. She took the Number 8 shirt and slotted straight into Arsenal's midfield – happy to play as a Number 10, a winger, or a deeper lying central midfielder.

Across the WSL season, her 14 goal involvements (nine goals and five assists) were more than all other players except Elisabeth Terland and Viviane Asseyi, while her 43 chances created was a total only beaten by Kate McCabe.

In recognition of her incredible season, Caldentey won Arsenal's Player of the Year award and the

Women's Professional Game's WSL Player of the Year.

'She's a total footballer,' said manager Renée Slegers. 'She's got everything.'

The recruitment team had been right. Caldentey was world class, and in May 2025 she showed that she could take Arsenal to the next level: she lifted the Champions League trophy!

 KYLIAN MBAPPÉ (PSG TO REAL MADRID, FREE TRANSFER)

Real Madrid had chased him for years. Now, finally, they had their man. When Mbappé pulled on their shirt for the first time at his official unveiling, 80,000 fans greeted him with greed in their eyes. Now, they would be invincible…

Or would they?

Because when the season started, there was a problem: Mbappé and Real Madrid struggled. At one stage, their new striker managed just three goals in 11 appearances and missed crucial penalties in defeats against Liverpool and Athletic Bilbao.

'I couldn't do any worse, so when you hit rock bottom you can only go up,' he said of those misses. 'I was thinking too much… when you overthink, you don't focus on your game.'

So he refocused – and clawed his way up from rock bottom to the very top! By the end of the season, Mbappé had put together one of the finest debut seasons of all time by any Real Madrid forward. With 42 goals in 55 games, he won the European Golden Shoe and La Liga's top scorer award: the 'Pichichi'.

This relationship took a bit of time, but now that it's clicked, we're about to see a whole new level to Mbappé and Real Madrid…

SETH BURKETT

LA LIGA

LA LIGA REVIEW

'Vamos!'

Lamine Yamal could barely contain his excitement as he walked through the doors of Barcelona's training ground.

'Vamos!' he shouted again – meaning 'Let's go!' in English – and then spotted Raphinha and Dani Olmo, who greeted their teammate with a warm hug and a couple of fist pumps.

Lamine was pumped up. Only a few weeks earlier, the Spanish star had been the talk of the football world, becoming the youngest ever player to take part in and win the Euros.

Now – after a short holiday – he was ready to take on his next challenge.

'How are you feeling, Lamine?' asked his new manager Hansi Flick, checking if the teenage winger might be tired after his summertime exertions for

Spain. 'I'm wondering if we should slowly ease you into the new season?'

Yamine looked up with wide-eyed amazement.

'I'm ready to help Barca get back to the top of La Liga, boss,' he replied, before adding with a grin: 'And I can't do that while sitting on the sidelines!'

Hansi shouldn't have been surprised. Ten years might have passed since Lamine first joined Barcelona, but he was still only 17. Like most young players, all Lamine wanted to do was play.

And so on 17 August 2024, a month after playing in the Euros final, Lamine carried on from where he left off in Germany, with his exquisite pass setting up Robert Lewandowski and Barca kicking off the season with victory over Valencia.

Far from being tired, Lamine played a pivotal part in each one of the early-season games. He bagged his first goal with a curling shot from outside the box to beat Athletic Club. He teed up Dani for the winner at Rayo Vallecano. Two more assists followed against Rayo Valladolid, a couple of goals at Girona, and another assist at Villareal.

'What a start to the season,' Raphinha said to Lamine after they had achieved their seventh league win in a row. 'But we all know the biggest test is still to come.'

For Barca, that could only mean one thing.

Real Madrid v Barcelona. The match known as 'El Clasico', pitting the two biggest rivals in world football against each other.

After making his debut at the age of just 15, Lamine had suffered several disappointments against Real. He never enjoyed losing, but losing to their arch-rivals was ten times worse.

He was determined that this time would be different, even at Real's home fortress – the Santiago Bernabéu. But it would be far from easy.

Madrid boasted superstar ballers such as Kylian Mbappé, Vinicius Jr and Jude Bellingham. The reigning La Liga champions were looking to extend their unbeaten run in the league to an extraordinary 43 games, which would equal the record set by Barcelona.

Hansi put his faith in youth for the big match; several players in the starting line-up had come through the club's academy, including Lamine. The youngsters loved to play a thrilling, fast-paced, high-energy style that terrorised opposition defences and, come the second half, it was Madrid's turn to be bamboozled.

Two goals in three minutes from Robert – one with his trusty right foot, the other a perfectly placed header – stunned the hosts.

'Not bad for someone more than twice your age,' the 36-year-old striker joked to Lamine.

Next it was Lamine's turn. As Raphinha surged forward and Madrid's defenders frantically tried to block his path, Lamine found himself in space on the right of the penalty box.

'Play me in!' he shouted to his captain, who threaded a perfectly timed through-ball.

So often accustomed to shooting with his left foot, Lamine showed he was just as dangerous with his right, rifling the ball into the roof of the net.

'Goooooooooaaaaaallllllll!'

He peeled away in celebration, pointing to his shirt and the name on his back.

Not that anyone would forget his name in a hurry.

Lamine had just become the youngest ever scorer in the history of 'El Clasico'. Another record to celebrate, but not before he'd watched Raphinha lob past the Real keeper Andriy Lunin to complete a famous 4–0 win and ensure that Barca could move six points clear of their rivals.

The players were in boisterous mood after the match, the dressing room a scene of noisy singing and enthusiastic dancing.

'What a night!' Raphinha said to Lamine. 'Imagine the parties back in Barcelona.'

'Hopefully the dancing is a bit better back home!' Lamine chuckled.

The celebrations – and the six-point lead – didn't last for long, though. Barca suffered an unexpected slump in form and, by the beginning of 2025, found themselves behind not just one team from Madrid but two – Real and their city rivals, Atlético.

Things grew worse off the field too. Lamine suffered two ankle injuries in a matter of weeks and had to miss several games.

Robert put a comforting arm around his shoulder.

'Remember, Lamine, it's a marathon, not a sprint,' he explained. 'There are always twists and turns in a league season – and there'll be plenty more to come.'

'Let's just hope there are no more twists of my ankle,' Lamine grimaced.

It was another match against Real that sparked Barca's return to form. This time, it was the Spanish Super Cup final, but the outcome was the same, with Barcelona smashing five past their opponents. Lamine, fit and firing once again, kicked off the rout with a delicious finish into the bottom corner.

From there, the goals – and the wins – kept on coming. Seven against Valencia, four away to Sevilla, another four against Real Sociedad. Barca were back in the title race and, by the time they travelled to Madrid in March for a crunch match against Atlético, things could not have been any closer.

Victory would see them leapfrog Real at the top; defeat, however, would hand the advantage to Atlético. And a loss looked very much on the cards with only 20 minutes remaining as the home side held a 2–0 lead.

'Keep going, boys,' keeper Wojciech Szczęsny urged

his teammates. 'One goal and we're right back in it.'

If anyone knew about comebacks, it was Wojciech. He had retired from football the previous summer, but was persuaded by Barcelona to put his gloves on again when first-choice keeper Marc-André ter Stegen suffered a serious injury.

With Wojciech's encouraging words spurring the team on, Robert leapt upon a half-chance in the area to reduce the deficit. One goal quickly became two when Ferran Torres nodded one home and, as the match entered added time, Atlético were hanging on for a draw.

Lamine was in no mood to settle for a point, though. Picking up the ball on the edge of the area, he jinked inside a defender before unleashing a left-foot drive into the corner, helped along the way by a deflection. Minutes later, another goal from Ferran put the result beyond doubt.

This courageous team had shown once again that they refused to be beaten – and they carried that confidence into the rest of the season.

This included another cup triumph against Real

Madrid, a thrilling 3–2 win after extra time in the Copa del Rey final. Different competition, same result – the only thing that was different was Lamine's hair, which was now a striking blonde.

'I dyed my hair because I was bored at home!' he revealed to reporters afterwards.

There was nothing boring about Barcelona's exhilarating football, though. And when they came face to face again with Madrid a couple of weeks later, they knew victory would put them within touching distance of the title.

Once again, they handed their opponents a two-goal head-start through Mbappé but, by half-time, they had hit back with four goals of their own, including another stunner from distance by Lamine. Mbappé completed his hat-trick but it wasn't enough.

For the first time since 1983, Barcelona had won four 'El Clasicos' in the same season, scoring a barely believable 16 goals in the process.

The only thing that could make it even more special was winning La Liga. That duly followed four days later, a routine 2–0 win over Espanyol ensuring they were crowned champions with two games to spare.

Lamine's long-range curler to open the scoring was yet another example of his extraordinary contribution to Barca's triumphant league season.

35 games, nine goals, 13 assists… and one change of hair colour.

LA LIGA FINAL TABLE

Pos	Team Name	Played	Wins	Draws	Losses	Goal Diff.	Points
1	**Barcelona**	**38**	**28**	**4**	**6**	**63**	**88**
2	Real Madrid	38	26	6	6	40	84
3	Atlético de Madrid	38	22	10	6	38	76
4	Athletic Club	38	19	13	6	25	70
5	Villarreal	38	20	10	8	20	70
6	Real Betis	38	16	12	10	7	60
7	Celta Vigo	38	16	7	15	2	55
8	Rayo Vallecano	38	13	13	12	-4	52
9	Osasuna	38	12	16	10	-4	52
10	Mallorca	38	13	9	16	-9	48
11	Real Sociedad	38	13	7	18	-11	46
12	Valencia	38	11	13	14	-10	46
13	Getafe	38	11	9	18	-5	42
14	Espanyol	38	11	9	18	-11	42
15	Alavés	38	10	12	16	-10	42
16	Girona	38	11	8	19	-16	41
17	Sevilla	38	10	11	17	-13	41
18	*Leganés*	*38*	*9*	*13*	*16*	*-17*	*40*
19	*Las Palmas*	*38*	*8*	*8*	*22*	*-21*	*32*
20	*Valladolid*	*38*	*4*	*4*	*30*	*-64*	*16*

LA LIGA TOP SCORERS

		Goals	Assists	Games
1	Kylian Mbappé	31	3	34
2	Robert Lewandowski	27	2	34
3	Ante Budimir	21	4	38
4	Alexander Sørloth	20	2	35
5	Ayoze Pérez	19	2	30
6	Raphinha	18	9	36
7	Julián Alvarez	17	4	37
8	Oihan Sancet	15	1	29
9	Kike García	13	0	35
10	Javier Puado	12	4	35

TOP 5 MANAGERS

These managers called the shots – and in some cases they won the lot. In a season of immense achievements from clubs around the world, here are five managers who were at the very top of their game.

 **1 NUNO ESPÍRITO SANTO**

How do you go from avoiding relegation on the final day of the 2023–24 season to playing for a place in the Champions League just 12 months later?

Answer: you give Nuno his first full season in charge of Nottingham Forest.

Yes, after finishing a lowly 17th in the 2023–24 season, many predicted that Forest would struggle once more. Perhaps they'd even be relegated?

Not with this manager! Nuno transformed his team through clever coaching. He gave them solid defensive foundations and a lethal counterattacking style. New signings Matz Sels and Nikola Milenković kept 13 clean sheets, Morgan Gibbs-White added sparkle, Anthony Elanga and Callum Hudson-Odoi gave pace, while Chris Wood bagged goals.

Though they lost out to Chelsea on the final day, Nuno's team still qualified for European football for the first time in 30 years!

2 LUIS ENRIQUE

Something incredible happened in Paris. Manager Luis Enrique made his PSG team… likeable.

And he also made them better! Yes, despite losing his best player (Kylian Mbappé), Enrique simply pressed the reset button. Instead of turning his PSG team into megastars, he intended to transform them into a young, hungry side willing to work for each other.

They'd become the fittest team in the world, and they'd also play the best, most entertaining football.

They would have the right attitude. There would be no big egos.

And with Enrique at the wheel, it worked beautifully.

PSG won their first ever Champions League and first ever quadruple. In doing so, Enrique became the seventh manager in history to win the Champions League with two different clubs, and just the second to win a treble with two different teams.

 SONIA BOMPASTOR

Across 12 years in charge at Chelsea, Emma Hayes won seven WSL titles, five FA Cups and two League Cups. She was undoubtedly the best coach in the English game.

So, when she announced her departure, Chelsea's rivals perked up. Perhaps this would be their opportunity? Surely Chelsea's new coach couldn't dream of being anywhere near as successful. Right...?

Wrong! Recruited from Lyon, Sonia Bompastor

made English football look easy as she swept aside all domestic competition.

She adapted to life in England so quickly that she set a record for the best-ever start to a WSL season, with seven wins out of seven.

Despite injuries to stars like Sam Kerr, Bompastor used her squad well, rotating players to keep them fresh and giving chances to promising youngsters.

And for that she was rewarded. Chelsea had lost their previous three League Cup finals, but with Bompastor in charge they beat Manchester City 2–1. They followed that up with a 3–0 FA Cup final win. But most impressively, they set a whole host of new records as they recorded an unbeaten WSL season, winning the league by a whopping 12 points!

RENÉE SLEGERS

Arsenal's stuttering start to the season in the WSL was simply not good enough. Under manager Jonas Eidevall, they had won just one of their four league matches and been hammered 5–2 by Bayern Munich.

Something major had to change and Eidevall knew what that had to be: he would quit as manager. But could interim Head Coach Renée Slegers, previously Eidevall's assistant, save their season?

Under Slegers' guidance, Arsenal won ten of their next 11 games (and drew the other one) and shot up the standings, eventually finishing as runners-up in the WSL.

But Slegers saved her finest work for the Champions League, where against all the odds her 'comeback queens' beat Real Madrid, European powerhouses Lyon and holders Barcelona to lift the trophy!

ANTONIO CONTE

After finishing 41 points behind Inter Milan in a failed title defence, Napoli needed to get back on track. And so, they recruited Antonio Conte as their new manager.

He may only have had the fifth highest wage bill in

the Italian league, but Conte set about proving that he is a serial winner. Since his first job in management he has won titles with every single club he's coached… except Tottenham!.

Conte recruited smartly, signing Romelu Lukaku, Billy Gilmour, Scott McTominay and David Neres.

He set clever tactics, instructing his team to press high and play with intensity.

And he got the best out of his players… particularly Scott McTominay.

Not even the sale of Khvicha Kvaratskhelia to PSG in January 2025 could stop Napoli, and Conte's men became champions on the final day of the season. In doing so, Conte became the first manager to win Serie A with three different clubs!

LIGUE 2

LIGUE 2 REVIEW

The Paris Saint-Germain squad for the 2024–25 season had a different feel to it.

In years gone by, the team could seem like a who's who of football's global superstars. There was Neymar, there was Lionel Messi, there was Kylian Mbappé – players who had won everything the game had to offer and were famous in every corner of the world.

PSG had dominated French football, winning 10 of the previous 12 Ligue 1 titles. Now – following Kylian's move to Real Madrid in the summer – all three stars had moved on, leaving many people wondering what PSG would do without them.

The answer?

Get even better!

Their squad might have had a fresh look but there was still no shortage of stardust. Two of the brightest young prospects in the game – new signings Désiré Doué and João Neves – were ready to slot in alongside more experienced figures such as Marquinhos, the team captain, keeper Gianluigi Donnarumma and World Cup winner Ousmane Dembélé.

For Ousmane, the new season posed an extra special challenge.

'Your task,' explained his manager Luis Enrique, 'is to fill a Kylian Mbappé-sized hole.'

'No pressure then, boss!' Ousmane grinned.

While he may have been smiling, Ousmane knew just how hard it would be to step into the shoes of his France teammate. Kylian had been named the Ligue 1 player of the season five years in a row.

But if he was daunted by the task, Ousmane didn't show it as he enjoyed a terrific start to the campaign. Four goals and three assists in the first six games helped propel the reigning champions to the top of the league.

Two of those goals came in a match-winning performance against Brest. With his team losing 1–0 in front of a disgruntled Parc des Princes crowd, Ousmane cheered everyone up before half-time when he nodded in an equaliser.

In the second half, he continued to torment his opponents down the right wing, eventually sealing the win when he was quickest to react to a blocked shot.

'Who needs Kylian?' Gianluigi joked with his teammate after the match.

It wasn't just Ousmane's attacking play that was making a difference. He was becoming a leader of the team – all over the pitch. When PSG didn't have the ball, he would run hard to press their opponents, desperate to win back possession. An inspiration to his teammates.

In such a positive environment, the younger players were thriving. Their fast-flowing football, which combined speed with skill, was thrilling to watch – unless you were on the other team.

At the end of October, PSG travelled to face title rivals Olympique Marseille, who were only three points adrift in the table.

The reigning champions made the gap look a lot bigger. By the time the referee blew his whistle for half-time, some of the Marseille fans had already left the Stade Vélodrome, with their team trailing 3–0 and down to ten men.

It took PSG just seven minutes to make the breakthrough, João finding the net from inside the box for his first goal for the club. A red card and an own goal minutes later made things even worse for the home side before Ousmane left his mark on the game.

Rampaging down the right wing into the penalty area, his fierce drive was well saved. As the ball rebounded to him, Ousmane leapt to his feet. With defenders rushing at him, he had a fraction of a second to collect his thoughts.

'Could I have another shot?' Ousmane wondered, despite it being a tight angle. 'Or should I …?'

Out of the corner of his eye, he had spotted Bradley Barcola.

A quick square pass across goal. A first-time shot from Bradley. 3–0!

PSG didn't score any more goals in the second half, but it didn't matter. The damage had been done, and they now held a six-point lead over Marseille.

Not that they could afford to relax. In Ligue 1, there was always another test around the corner.

Just before Christmas, it was high-flying Monaco's turn to try to topple PSG, who were playing a fearsome front three of Ousmane, Désiré and Bradley.

Another routine win appeared on the cards when Désiré opened the scoring with a sweet finish to record his first goal for the club.

'I'm sure that'll be the first of many, mate,' Bradley said as he congratulated his teammate.

However, two quickfire goals from Monaco in the second half turned the match around. PSG had not lost any of their first 15 league games, but their unbeaten record was under serious threat.

'Come on, boys. It's not over yet. Let's keep going,' Ousmane urged his teammates.

He knew he had to lead by example and, when a shot was parried in the box, it was Ousmane who reacted fastest, sweeping home an equaliser.

It was just the spark that PSG needed. Substitute Gonçalo Ramos headed the league leaders in front, then – as Monaco poured forward chasing a third goal – Ousmane took advantage of the space at the back to break clear, dinking the ball into the net with his left foot.

Luis was delighted with how Ousmane was responding to his new responsibilities. As well as showing his leadership qualities, he was no longer just a dazzling winger, but had also become a free-scoring central striker, lethal with both feet and his head.

Luis was also thrilled with how the whole team was gelling. By early February, after they plundered nine goals in the return matches against Brest and Monaco – with Ousmane grabbing five! – PSG had stretched their lead to a massive 13 points.

A fourth Ligue 1 title in a row was already within touching distance, and a run of ten straight league wins put the result beyond any doubt.

With six games still remaining, the new-look PSG team wrapped up the league title with victory over Angers. Fittingly, Désiré, one of their new stars, scored the only goal – an eye-catching volley at the far post.

It was a season of complete domination. They scored 92 goals on their way to winning the league by 19 points, and only lost their first game in late April when the league title had long since been wrapped up.

Ousmane's 21 goals made him the joint top scorer in Ligue 1. Speaking to reporters, he explained that his success was down to hard work.

'Now, even on my days off, I like to go to the training centre, recover, work with the physios,' he revealed. 'Before, I would go home, play NBA 2K, watch a bit of TV.'

The hard work had paid off in spectacular fashion. At the end of the season, Ousmane was announced as the Ligue 1 player of the season, following in the footsteps of his old teammate. That Kylian Mbappé hole had definitely been filled.

FRANCE FINAL TABLE

Pos	Team Name	Played	Wins	Draws	Losses	Goal Diff.	Points
1	**FC Lorient**	**34**	**22**	**5**	**7**	**37**	**71**
2	Paris FC	34	21	6	7	22	39
3	Metz	34	18	11	5	30	65
4	Dunkerque	34	17	5	12	7	56
5	Guingamp	34	17	4	13	12	55
6	Annecy	34	14	9	11	-1	51
7	Slade Laval	34	14	8	12	6	50
8	Bastia	34	11	15	8	6	48
9	Grenoble Foot 38	34	13	7	14	-1	46
10	Troyes	34	13	5	16	2	44
11	Amiens SC	34	13	4	17	-12	43
12	Ajaccio	34	12	6	16	-12	42
13	Pau	34	10	12	12	-14	42
14	Rodez	34	9	12	13	2	39
15	Red Star	34	9	11	14	-14	38
16	Clermont Foot	34	7	12	15	-16	33
17	*Martigues*	*34*	*9*	*5*	*20*	*-27*	*32*
18	*Caen*	*34*	*5*	*7*	*22*	*-27*	*22*

	FRANCE TOP SCORERS	Goals	Assists	Games
1	Éli Kroupi	22	3	30
2=	Jean-Philippe Krasso	17	5	31
2=	Timothé Nkada	17	5	31
4	Cheikh Sabaly	18	3	33
5	Sambou Soumano	14	3	32
6	Gauthier Hein	12	6	33
7	Malik Sellouki	11	4	33
8=	Jacques Siwe	11	2	28
8=	Antoine Leautey	10	4	34
10	Pape Meïssa Ba	10	2	18

TOP 5 CRAZIEST MOMENTS

Wouldn't it be weird if football was... normal? From ghostly goings-on to humble hot takes, these five moments had us scratching our heads.

1. LADS, PLEASE STOP SCORING!

Nottingham Forest's whopping 7–0 victory over Brighton sent *almost* all of their fans into seventh heaven. For Beccy Webster, though, landlady of Nottinghamshire pub The Gedling Inn, it was a bittersweet afternoon...

To get punters into her pub, she had decided to offer a free pint to everyone for every goal Nottingham Forest scored that afternoon.

Uh-oh...

'When the final whistle went, I just said "phew",' Beccy said after handing out the last of the 300 free drinks. Sounds like thirsty work!

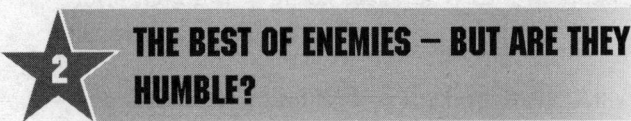

THE BEST OF ENEMIES – BUT ARE THEY HUMBLE?

'You want a war? Now we war,' announced Manchester City manager Pep Guardiola after his team's feisty encounter against ten-man Arsenal in September 2024.

Their first battle had ended in a dishonourable draw. Though there were no actual beheadings, there was plenty of 'headloss'.

Leandro Trossard was sent off deep into first-half stoppage time, while Erling Haaland and Gabriel Magalhães clashed throughout. When John Stones dramatically equalised late on, Haaland celebrated by picking the ball out of the net and bouncing it off Gabriel's head!

And he wasn't done there… at the full-time whistle, Haaland sought out Arsenal manager Mikel Arteta and told him to 'stay humble'.

Wow, now Arsenal were riled up!

So when they faced off in the return leg, Arsenal were desperate to win. After going 1–0 up, Gabriel celebrated in Haaland's face. And when Myles Lewis-Skelly scored to make it 3–1, he mocked Haaland by performing the Norwegian's famous yoga meditation celebration. Ouch!

Haaland was humbled as Arsenal triumphed 5–1, and there was still time for one final humiliation. At full-time, Arsenal's PA system blared out the song 'Humble' by Kendrick Lamar!

HOLLOWAY HAUNTED!

League Two side Swindon Town appointed Ian Holloway as their new boss in October 2024. Unfortunately, he didn't make the best of starts. His side went five games without a league win. But as fans and journalists queued up to question his tactics, Holloway gave a simple explanation for their poor form: the training ground was haunted.

'There's a graveyard near here. Honestly, I'm not joking,' he said. 'There's some strange things happening.'

Holloway called in special help from his wife, who waved sage around in an attempt to cleanse the training ground.

The ghosts must have taken a little time to leave – Swindon lost their next three games. But then, suddenly, their form turned! In the space of a month they beat Fleetwood, Wycombe, Grimsby and Colchester.

From 22nd place in the league, Swindon were suddenly soaring into mid-table. They finished the season in 12th place – safe from relegation, and from the spooky spirits!

4 A SLICE OF MISFORTUNE

Ipswich defender Axel Tuanzebe doesn't always do normal. Yes, he's a Premier League footballer, but also a Hungry, Hungry Hippos Guinness World Record holder. Yet both careers were put at risk after Tuanzebe suffered a serious injury in October 2024.

So how did he do it? Was it a bad tackle at the training ground, a high-impact collision?

No, he was washing up.

A jagged glass sliced Tunazebe's thumb so badly that he needed surgery!

'I'm just grateful that I still have my thumb intact,' the full-back said.

And that wasn't the season's only strange injury… Former West Ham boss Julen Lopetegui managed to pull his calf muscle in September – by stamping on the ground in anger! His Hammers team were losing 5–1 to Liverpool in fairness… The injury was so bad that Lopetetgui had to leave the stadium on crutches!

'I can't play in the next match,' he joked in his post-match press conference.

5. SACKED FOR A BIG MAC

Kristoffer Klaesson was once a promising goalkeeper for Leeds United, playing three games for the Yorkshire club and even keeping a clean sheet in a Premier League fixture. But with his career never quite taking off, Leeds accepted an offer for their Norwegian shotstopper from Polish side Raków Częstochowa.

A promising new start? Well, when Klaesson checked in for pre-season there was a problem: the club believed that Klaesson was out of shape and overweight.

Klaesson was banished to the reserves and ordered to lose eight kilograms of weight. But he had other ideas, and when he was spotted by fans in fast-food restaurant McDonald's, his new employers were livid.

Within weeks, Klaesson's contract had been torn up and he was on the move again – this time to Danish club AGF Aarhus.

SCOTTISH PREMIER LEAGUE

SCOTTISH PREMIER LEAGUE REVIEW

It was the first day of pre-season training and Brendan Rodgers was giving his Celtic team a history lesson.

'Fifty-five – that is the magic number, boys.'

The manager looked around at the faces staring back at him, a few of them wearing puzzled expressions.

'Anyone know what I'm referring to?' he asked.

'I would say your age, boss, but I know you can't be a year older than forty!' joked captain Callum McGregor.

Brendan, who had turned 50 the previous year, let out a little chuckle before continuing: 'If we win the Scottish Premiership this season, it will be league title Number 55. And that will mean we finally draw level with that lot across the city.'

Now all the players knew exactly what he was talking about. Separated by just four miles across

Glasgow, Celtic and 'that lot' – otherwise known as Rangers – had been ferocious rivals for more than a century, regularly tussling to be the top team in Scotland. And while both sides had held the upper hand at different points, it was Rangers who could boast the most league titles – a record they had held for almost a century. However, after being crowned champions 12 times in the previous 13 seasons, Celtic – with 54 titles – were catching up quickly.

Kasper Schmeichel was certainly enjoying the lesson. The Denmark captain had signed for Celtic in the summer and was keen to learn as much as possible about his new club.

One person he already knew well was Brendan, who had been his manager at Leicester City when they won the FA Cup.

'Nice to have the dream team back together, boss,' Kasper said with a smile after signing his contract.

Kasper had carved out a reputation as one of the world's best goalkeepers, wearing the gloves for several top clubs across Europe and starring for Denmark at the World Cup and Euros. Most famously, he had played a central role in Leicester's fairytale Premier League triumph in 2016.

'There's one thing you'll need to get used to here,' Brendan explained to his new signing. 'At Leicester, winning the league was the most incredible surprise... at Celtic, the fans expect it.'

That suited Kasper just fine. He was in the twilight of his career and hungry to win more trophies. His determination quickly became clear to everyone at the club.

In the first six league games, the keeper didn't concede a single goal. What's more, Celtic won all of them. The run included a 3–0 thrashing of Rangers, sparked by a cool close-range finish from star striker Daizen Maeda, then a second goal on the stroke of half-time from Kyōgo Furuhashi. Callum's breathtaking strike from the edge of the box put the game to bed.

After keeping out the Bhoys' opponents for 533 minutes, Kasper finally conceded his first league goal against Ross County. Even that only came from a retaken penalty after the Dane had saved the first effort but was adjudged to have moved too early.

Celtic went on to win the match, yet Kasper was not best pleased. He never liked conceding goals.

'Don't worry, mate,' Callum said. 'Put all your frustration into a great performance in our next match – that's the big one.'

The 'big one' would be against Aberdeen. Like Celtic, the Dons had won all seven league games so far, meaning both teams came into the clash at Parkhead with 100 per cent records.

An eighth win seemed inevitable for Celtic when first-half goals from Reo Hatate and Kyōgo put the Bhoys in control. Yet Aberdeen responded in stunning fashion, drawing level with two quick-fire strikes, and even had a potential winner ruled out by VAR.

This time, it wasn't just Kasper who was annoyed after the match; the whole team were in disbelief that they'd thrown away a two-goal lead, not to mention their perfect record. But Brendan wasn't going to let anyone start sulking.

'Chin up, lads,' Brendan encouraged his team. 'One winning run has come to an end. Let's get back out there and start another one.'

The team talk worked. With Kasper in fine form between the sticks, Celtic won their next five league games, conceding just one goal along the way, before travelling to Aberdeen in December.

What was already a tough challenge was made even harder by the wet, cold and windy weather in the north-east of Scotland. Conditions that made life tricky for Kasper, who had to react sharply to keep out an effort from Luis Lópes in the first half.

'Smart save, keeps,' said Callum.

'You know how much I like a clean sheet, skipper.' Kasper smiled.

Another stalemate seemed inevitable before a moment of magic from Greg Taylor played in Reo, who chested the ball down before firing home with his left foot.

The final whistle prompted jubilant celebrations from the Celtic players – not just because they could return to a warm, dry dressing room. The result moved them seven points clear of Aberdeen.

From that magical season at Leicester, Kasper knew what it was like to be the frontrunners and had some wise words for his teammates.

'This is when we need to dig deep and raise our game even higher, boys. We are the team everyone wants to beat,' he told his teammates.

Of course, no football club wanted to beat Celtic more than Rangers, and the two sides faced off later that month in the Scottish League Cup final. A frantic end-to-end battle, where the lead changed hands several times, finally finished 3–3. The match would be decided by penalties.

Kasper loved a shootout. Being a keeper, it gave him the chance to be the hero, and so it proved when he saved Ridvan Yilmaz's effort, paving the way for Daizen to score the winning penalty. Another blow struck against their rivals; another trophy for the cabinet.

'I could get used to this,' a smiling Kasper told Daizen, as he looked down at the gleaming medal around his neck.

At the start of the new year, Rangers got some revenge, ending Celtic's unbeaten league run. Yet the Bhoys again showed their ability to bounce back: only three days later, a win against St Mirren extended their lead to a massive 13 points.

From that point, there was no turning back. Even with several months of the season remaining, Celtic had far too much experience and ability to let their advantage slip. Inspired by Daizen's 16 goals and 10 assists in the league, the runaway leaders continued to bulldoze their opponents.

A shoulder injury suffered in March ruled Kasper out of the title run-in, including the 5–0 thumping of Dundee United that sealed the title but, fittingly, he returned for the final match against St Mirren – just in time for the trophy-lifting celebrations.

Ninety-two points, 112 goals, a fourth league title in a row, and also their 13th title in 14 seasons. The first time Celtic had drawn level with Rangers for 95 years.

And for Kasper, there was one personal stat that didn't make as many headlines but was no less important. He had kept 19 clean sheets in the league. No wonder he was smiling when he hoisted the Premiership trophy into the air.

SPL FINAL TABLE

Pos	Team Name	Played	Wins	Draws	Losses	Goal Diff.	Points
1	**Celtic**	**38**	**29**	**5**	**4**	**86**	**92**
2	Rangers	38	22	9	7	39	75
3	Hibernian	38	15	13	10	12	58
4	Dundee United	38	15	8	15	-9	53
5	Aberdeen	38	15	8	15	-13	53
6	St. Mirren	38	14	8	16	-6	50
7	Hearts	38	15	7	16	5	52
8	Motherwell	38	14	7	17	-17	49
9	Kilmarnock	38	12	8	18	-19	44
10	Dundee	38	11	8	19	-20	41
11	Ross County	38	9	10	19	-28	37
12	*St. Johnstone*	*38*	*9*	*5*	*24*	*-30*	*32*

SPL TOP SCORERS

		Goals	Assists	Games
1	Daizen Maeda	16	7	30
2	Simon Murray	15	3	33
3	Sam Dalby	14	2	30
4=	Cyriel Dessers	12	2	30
4=	Martin Boyle	11	5	31
6	Václav Černý	11	2	28
7=	Hamza Igamane	11	1	29
7=	Nicolas Kühn	10	8	28
9	Kyōgo Furuhashi	10	3	22
10=	Arne Engels	9	5	30

TOP 5 INCREDIBLE MOMENTS

Football is a game of highs, lows, and unbelievable moments. Fans gasp, commentators scream, and clips go viral as minnows overcome giants, records are broken, and new legends are made. If Hollywood scriptwriters were working on the 2024–25 season, these are five of the best stories they'd have come up with...

1 A SHOW FOR GOODISON

After 133 years, Everton played their final season at Goodison Park. To celebrate, they took part in some memorable home matches. They saved their most dramatic, however, for Goodison's last Merseyside derby.

Played under the floodlights, the game was a

topsy-turvy affair. Everton took a 1–0 lead, only for Liverpool to turn the game around with two devastating goals. As the clock ticked past 90 minutes, it seemed that Everton fans were going to leave Goodison Park disappointed.

But then, defender James Tarkowski smashed in a 98th minute volley! Cue pandemonium as Goodison erupted. It may only have been a 2–2 draw, but such a sweet finish felt like a dramatic, historic win – a fitting tribute to a wonderful stadium!

 2 WHAT'S HE DOING UP THERE?

Thirty-seven-year-old Francesco Acerbi had never scored a European goal. The fact that the Italian defender was even on the pitch was incredible enough. He'd almost retired from football in his 20s, and twice overcame cancer.

Now, he was fighting for his Inter Milan side, who were finding themselves 3–2 down against Barcelona in the Champions League semi-final. There were just minutes left – and Inter were heading for elimination.

So Acerbi moved up front. He may have been a defender, but when Denzel Dumfries's cross fell to him in the box, he finished like a striker. Goal!

Acerbi had done it: he'd scored a dramatic injury time equaliser to take the game to extra time (which Inter would also win!).

'I thank him for finding the strength to go into the box at that moment,' said his delighted teammate Carlos Augusto.

THAT'S A BOLD CLAIM, MATE

In August 2024, Spurs boss Ange Postecoglou made an announcement: 'Usually in my second season, I win things.'

Hmm, hadn't the Australian checked Spurs' recent trophy record? They hadn't won a single title since the League Cup in 2008 – and that had been their only win in the 21st century!

In that time, world-class players like Luka Modrić and Harry Kane had tried and failed to succeed. Managers who always won, like José Mourinho and Antonio Conte, had also tried and failed with Spurs. Losing had become 'Spursy'. The club, many believed, was cursed.

But in September, Ange doubled down on his statement. 'I'll correct myself,' he said. 'I don't usually win things, I *always* win things in my second year.'

Wow! His bold claim began to look ridiculous as Spurs slid down the Premier League. In the FA Cup they needed extra time to beat National League side Tamworth before losing their fourth round match against Aston Villa. In the League Cup they beat Liverpool 1–0 in their semi-final first leg… only to be hammered 4–0 in the second leg.

That left the Europa League as their only hope!

While Ange's team had been terrible in the Premier League (losing 22 games!), they'd been impressive in the Europa League. After triumphing in the semi-finals, they faced Manchester United in the final… and won!

Ange had been telling the truth. He'd won in his second season! As his Spurs players celebrated on the pitch, James Maddison and Sergio Reguilón unfurled a flag. It was a meme of Ange in sunglasses, bearing the iconic words: I ALWAYS win things in my second year.

 4 THE BLACK CATS ARE BACK

Not even the Hollywood scriptwriters could have come up with this storyline. Ever since their relegation from the Premier League in 2017, Sunderland fans had suffered from far more downs than ups – including their relegation to League One.

Many of the downs were captured in the documentary *Sunderland 'Til I Die*, which ran for three seasons on Netflix. But after the cameras stopped rolling and the scriptwriters left Sunderland, something strange happened… the Black Cats improved!

In fact, they improved so much that they made the Championship play-offs. Little did they know, the drama was only just beginning.

Despite finishing fourth, Sunderland had lost their last five league matches. But in the play-offs, they turned the form book on its head.

In the semi-final second leg, a header from Dan Ballard in the last minute of extra-time gave them a 3–2 aggregate win over Coventry City.

And in the final they repeated the trick: Tommy Watson scored a long-range 95th minute winner as Sunderland came back from 1–0 down to beat Sheffield United 2–1. They had returned to the Premier League in the most spectacular of circumstances!

THE YEAR OF THE UNDERDOG

We love football for the drama. Anyone can beat anyone. Minnows can overcome giants. Legends can be made… especially in cup competitions!

TOP 5 INCREDIBLE MOMENTS

This year we were treated to plenty of upsets...

In the FA Cup: Plymouth beat Liverpool... fifth-tier Tamworth took Tottenham Hotspur to extra time... part-time Harborough took Reading to extra time... seventh-tier Kettering Town beat local rivals Northampton... and, of course, Crystal Palace beat Manchester City in the final.

... in the women's Champions League final Arsenal beat Barcelona...

... Aberdeen beat Celtic in the Scottish Cup final...

... and Peterborough United beat big-spending Birmingham in the EFL trophy!

SETH BURKETT

CHAMPIONS LEAGUE

CHAMPIONS LEAGUE REVIEW

Désiré Doué looked around the packed stands of the Allianz Arena, trying not to be overawed by the enormity of the occasion.

More than 64,000 supporters in the Munich stadium – and many millions around the world – were about to watch him play in the biggest game in club football.

The Champions League final.

In such an atmosphere, even the game's most experienced players could be forgiven for feeling some nerves, let alone a 19-year-old who had never played in the Champions League before this season and only scored his first goal for Paris Saint-Germain in December.

Désiré took a deep breath. It was time to show the world what he could do.

Six months earlier, the chances of PSG making it to Munich seemed about as likely as the England cricket team reaching the Rugby World Cup final. After some disappointing displays in the league phase, there was a genuine possibility that the reigning Ligue 1 champions might suffer the embarrassment of not qualifying for the knockout rounds.

PSG finally found form in a crucial clash with Manchester City, showing their fighting spirit to overturn a two-goal deficit and record a vital win. From there, having already dispatched one English side, they single-handedly shattered the Champions League dreams of the Premier League's top clubs.

Liverpool in the last 16? A nail-biting tie went all the way to a penalty shootout, where Gianluigi Donnarumma's two saves paved the way for Désiré to slot home the winning kick.

Aston Villa in the quarter-finals? Another close encounter, but the French side did enough to squeak through 5–4 on aggregate.

Arsenal in the semi-finals? The same story but this time a more comfortable margin of victory.

'It's a shame there are no English teams left for the final,' Désiré joked with Ousmane Dembélé as they celebrated reaching the Champions League decider.

Ousmane had taken on a starring role in the competition following the departure of superstar Kylian Mbappé to Real Madrid, with his eight goals propelling the team to the final.

Of course, the PSG players knew whoever they faced would be a quality opponent – English or not – and they didn't come much more formidable than Inter Milan. Finalists in 2023, the Italian giants had already knocked out Bayern Munich and Barcelona. Now they were relishing the opportunity to add the scalp of the French champions.

While PSG were hunting a first Champions League trophy, Inter were three-time champions. They had the advantage of experience too, with the likes of Francesco Acerbi, Henrikh Mkhitaryan and keeper Yann Sommer, all veterans of European competition.

PSG's team, on the other hand, was on average five years younger.

'Hanging out with you lot makes me feel old,' Ousmane – not exactly a veteran at 28! – would joke with Désiré and his young teammates Bradley Barcola and Senny Mayulu at training.

Yet what they might have lacked in experience, they more than made up for in energy – and from the very first minute, the French side tore into their opponents.

Stringing together some slick passing moves and delightful touches, they posed an immediate attacking threat. And when they didn't have the ball, they did everything they could to win it back, not allowing Inter any time in possession.

An early breakthrough seemed inevitable and, after 12 minutes, PSG duly struck the first blow. Ghosting into space in the penalty area, Désiré collected a pass with his left foot before twirling onto his right and threading a pass across goal to set up a simple finish for Achraf Hakimi.

Any nerves that Désiré was feeling instantly vanished. He had just become the youngest ever player to create an assist in the Champions League final and was loving every minute of it.

Now full of confidence, PSG poured forward again and again. With only 20 minutes on the clock, they struck again after moving the ball the entire length of the field.

Picking up the ball from an Inter corner and showing no fear of conceding possession, Khvicha Kvaratskhelia drove forward. He found Ousmane, sprinting down the left wing,

'Switch it, Ousmane. I'm free!' Désiré shouted, trying to make himself heard over the din of the screaming fans.

Controlling the pass with his chest, Désiré unleashed a first-time shot, which took a deflection and beat Sommer at the near post.

2–0!

Désiré spun away to celebrate in front of the fans, pulling off a perfectly executed knee slide.

'Nine out of 10 marks for the goal... 10 out of 10 for the knee slide!' Ousmane laughed.

Inter were shellshocked, their pre-match game plan already in tatters. With PSG unleashing 13 shots in the first half, the Italian side deserved credit for keeping the scoreline at 2–0.

Not that PSG coach Luis Enrique was letting his players take anything for granted.

'Some of you were in the team that lost in the semi-final last year,' he told his players at half-time. 'I don't want any of you to feel that pain again. Let's go out there and finish the job.'

Fired up by the team talk, the players carried on where they had left off in the first half, with Khvicha hitting the woodwork after just 39 seconds.

'Keep pushing, boys,' Luis encouraged his team from the sidelines.

Désiré was pulling out all the skills from his box of tricks, a flick here, a dummy there.

In the 63rd minute, Ousmane took a leaf out of his teammate's book, his cheeky backheel putting Vitinha in space in Inter's half. As Vitinha sprinted forward, Désiré peeled away to the right.

'Play it!' he yelled.

At the perfect moment, Vitinha delivered the pass to Désiré who – without breaking stride – hit a cool right-foot finish to beat Sommer.

Désiré had scored twice in the Champions League final. The youngest-ever player in history to do so.

There was no knee slide to celebrate this time;

instead he ripped off his shirt and flung it in the air.

With a 3–0 lead, PSG were now in complete control, but they weren't done yet. The rampaging Khvicha ran clear to net a deserved fourth goal before Senny – who had only come on as a sub a few minutes earlier – finished off another beautiful move.

PSG's first-ever Champions League win was in fact the biggest-ever winning margin in a final.

For Inter, it was a cruel end to a brilliant campaign, but there was no doubt that the best team had emerged victorious.

And there was no doubt about the game's best player either. For his two goals, one assist and 41 majestic touches, Désiré was named player of the match. No one should have been surprised – after all, his name when translated into English means 'Desire gifted'.

Club Brugge	1
Aston Villa	6

Paris Saint-Germain	1 (4)
Liverpool	1 (1)

Real Madrid	2 (4)
Atlético Madrid	2 (2)

PSV Eindhoven	3
Arsenal	9

Aston Villa	4
Paris Saint-Germain	5

Arsenal	5
Real Madrid	1

Paris Saint-Germain	3
Arsenal	1

Paris Saint-Germain	5
Inter Milan	0

Barcelona	6
Inter Milan	7

Borussia Dortmund	3
Barcelona	5

Bayern Munich	3
Inter Milan	4

Benfica	1
Barcelona	4

Borussia Dortmund	3
Lille	2

Bayern Munich	5
Bayer Leverkusen	0

Feyenoord	1
Inter Milan	4

CHAMPIONS LEAGUE TOP SCORERS

		Goals	Assists	Games
1=	Serhou Guirassy	13	2	14
1=	Raphinha	13	0	14
3=	Robert Lewandowski	11	1	13
3=	Harry Kane	11	0	13
3=	Lautaro Martínez	9	4	14
6=	Erling Haaland	8	0	9
6=	Vinicius Junior	8	0	12
6=	Ousmane Dembélé	8	2	15
6=	Kylian Mbappé	7	1	14
6=	Julián Alvarez	7	0	10
6=	Jonathan David	7	2	10
6=	Vangelis Pavlidis	7	1	12

TOP 5 PLAYERS

They say that there is no 'i' in team, but these 'i'ndividual players were at the top of their game during the 2024–25 season, making their teams so much better. Is it time for a new name on the Ballon d'Or? These players certainly think so…

1 ALESSIA RUSSO

Arsenal had already tried to sign her for a world record fee in January 2023. Instead, they had to wait until that summer to get their top target.

She was worth the wait.

In her debut season she scored 16 goals in 31 appearances. But in her second season, she lifted her game to a whole new level.

Russo won the FWA's Player of the Season award and finished as the WSL's joint top scorer, while her seven Champions League goals placed her second in the overall rankings, in joint position with teammate Mariona Caldentey. No English player had ever scored more goals in a single season of the women's Champions League.

And what important goals she scored! Two goals to spark Arsenal's immense comeback against Real Madrid in the quarter-final, followed by a goal and an assist in their 4–1 victory over Lyon in the semi-final.

'Under Slegers, her game has been elevated,' said former England forward Ellen White. 'Alessia's work ethic is phenomenal.' As is her movement, her hold-up play and her pressing!

2 RAPHINHA

He was good when he played for Leeds United, but nobody expected him to ever become *this* good.

With 34 goals and 25 assists in 57 games, Raphinha recorded a ridiculously good season as Barcelona won a domestic treble. In the moments when his side needed him, he produced with his lethal left foot: his 21 goal contributions in the Champions League equalled Cristiano's 2013–14 record, while he bagged vital goals against Benfica, Inter Milan and Real Madrid.

And yet Raphinha's wonderful season nearly didn't happen. With Barcelona in the market to sign Nico Williams, new coach Hansi Flick had to persuade Raphinha to remain at the club.

The deal fell through, Raphinha stayed, and for that Flick was rewarded. 'I have never had a player like him,' Flick purred – even handing Raphinha the captain's armband on 19 occasions.

'I would give the Ballon d'Or to Raphinha; Lamine Yamal would also give it to him!' said his teammate Pau Cubarsí.

LAMINE YAMAL

He's undoubtedly the best young player in the world. But is he also the best player in the world? Pau Cubarsí may back Raphinha, but plenty believe that Yamal is already the world's greatest.

The teenager has won every domestic trophy in Spain. He's a European champion with Spain. A World Cup and a Champions League, both of which seem very possible, would mean that he's completed football.

We've already learned of his big game moments in the Champions League, but Yamal also made the difference in each of his side's four victories over Real Madrid. He scored 17 and assisted 20 goals in 52 appearances, completing far more dribbles than any other player in La Liga (145), and creating 64 chances for his teammates.

The CIES Football Observatory calculated Yamal's value at £340 million, almost double that of second placed Erling Haaland (£200 million)!

MOHAMMED SALAH

At 32 years old, the Liverpool legend was supposed to start winding down. Instead, the wing wizard managed a whirlwind season of goals, assists, and victories to cement himself as one of the world's best.

With 29 Premier League goals he bagged a record-equalling fourth Golden Boot in five seasons. But in the 2024–25 season, Salah wasn't all about goals. Oh no, his all-round contribution reached new heights. His 18 assists were enough to secure him the Premier League's Playmaker Award for the first time, while the 29 clear-cut chances he created for his teammates also made him a league-leading figure.

Combined, Salah's 47 goal contributions is the joint-highest figure for a single season in Premier League history – and the highest ever for a 38-game season.

'This is my best season because I have made other players around me better,' he said.

Premier League and FWA officials agreed, as they voted him the Player of the Season. But most importantly, Salah's epic performances pushed his Liverpool side to their first Premier League trophy since 2019!

OUSMANE DEMBÉLÉ

There's never been any question over Dembélé's remarkable talent. Which is exactly why Barcelona paid £135.5 million for him back in 2017, at the time making him the second most expensive footballer in history.

But until 2025, Dembélé had never quite lived up to the hype.

So what happened? Manager Luis Enrique moved Dembélé from his preferred wing position to play as a striker.

Bang! Dembélé sparked into life. Suddenly, he played with freedom as attacks formed around him. He was central to Champions League victories over Liverpool and Arsenal, developing a lethal streak in front of goal. He scored 18 goals in just 11 appearances and would finish the season with eight goals and six assists in the Champions League, while contributing 21 goals and six assists in Ligue 1.

At Barcelona he was branded a 'waste of money' as he was sold to PSG for just £43.5 million. Yet within two seasons in France, the dangerous dribbler became a leading contender for the Ballon d'Or, winning the Champions League Player of the Season and Ligue 1's Player of the Year.

'I would give the Ballon d'Or to Mr Ousmane Dembélé,' said Enrique after their Champions League final success. 'The way he defended tonight, just that alone could be worth the Ballon d'Or.'

ACTIVITIES

ANAGRAMS

Can you unscramble these names of some of the top football players from the WSL? Test your knowledge!

C L Boy run ez _____

I W Real Kash _____

Nue Lame Jars _____

See Ergel Ren _____

Marem I Rez Ray _____

More Salt Bin Day _____

If A Man A Druma _____

A Sassio Rules _____

Leechy Lock _____

Melodic Human Rye _____

Italy Romance Dane _____

Bad Theme _____

QUIZ TIME!

Time to put your football knowledge to the test. See how many questions you can answer to find out if you're an ultimate football master!

1 Which iconic player held a young Lamine Yamal?
A. Christiano Ronaldo
B. Luka Modrić
C. Lionel Messi
D. David Beckham

2 What was the final score in the FA Cup Final 2024–25?
A. 3–2 to Crystal Palace
B. 2–1 to Manchester City
C. 2–1 to Crystal Palace
D. 1–0 to Crystal Palace

3 How many wins did Bayern have at the end of the Bundesliga 2024–25?
A. 20 wins
B. 30 wins
C. 25 wins
D. 15 wins

4 Roughly how many supporters fit into Munich Stadium?
A. 16,000
B. 128,000
C. 32,000
D. 64,000

5 In the Premier League match against Fulham, who did Bukayo Saka substitute in for on the pitch?
A. Mikel Merino
B. Declan Rice
C. Ethan Nwaneri
D. Martin Ødegaard

6 Before the 2024–25 season, what year was the last time Arsenal went beyond the quarter final stage of the Champions League?
A. 2008–9
B. 2003–4
C. 2011–14
D. 2000–01

7 Who is the 2024–25 goal keeper for Real Madrid?

A. Thibaut Courtois

B. Jan Oblak

C. Ederson

D. Emiliano Martínez

8 Who is the 2024–25 captain for Newcastle United?

A. Alexander Isak

B. William Osula

C. Kieran Trippier

D. Bruno Guimarães

9 Which team won the Women's Champions League Final 2024–25?

A. Barcelona

B. Real Madrid

C. Arsenal

D. Lyon

10 Which Tottenham defender accidentally tapped the ball into his own net in a match against Liverpool?
   A. Radu Drăguşin
   B. Kevin Danso
   C. Destiny Udogie
   D. Pedro Porro

11 In the Champions League Final between Arsenal and Barcelona, how many defensive actions did Leah Williamson perform?
   A. 15   C. 21
   B. 24   D. 19

12 How many years was Emma Hayes in charge of Chelsea?
   A. 15 years
   B. 8 years
   C. 12 years
   D. 2 years

13 Who is the captain for the 2024–25 Arsenal team?
A. Martin Ødegaard
B. Bukayo Saka
C. Declan Rice
D. Gabriel Martinelli

14 Which new signing below did Liverpool have for the 2024–25 season?
A. Mikel Merino
B. Riccardo Calafiori
C. Federico Chiesa
D. Kepa Arrizabalaga

15 Who was the player of the 2024–25 season of Ligue 1?
A. Kylian Mbappé
B. Ousmane Dembélé
C. Mason Greenwood
D. Désiré Doué

16 What team does midfielder Sandro Tonali play for in the 2024–25 Season?

A. Manchester United

B. AC Milan

C. Chelsea

D. Newcastle United

17 Who is the captain of Arsenal in WSL in the 2024–25 season?

A. Chloe Kelly

B. Kim Little

C. Alessia Russo

D. Leah Williamson

18 In his debut season at Chelsea, who scored four goals in a single game against Everton, with the final score as 6–0?

A. Tino Anjorin

B. Cole Palmer

C. Marc Guiu

D. Christopher Nkunku

19 What was the final score of the nail-biting Europa League quarter-final between Manchester United and Lyon?
A. 2–1
B. 1–0
C. 4–3
D. 5–4

20 Who scored the final header in that match?
A. Amad Diallo
B. Bruno Fernandes
C. Harry Maguire
D. Rasmus Højlund

21 What was the final score for the UEFA Champions League 2024–25 final?
A. 5–0
B. 3–1
C. 2–0
D. 4–3

22 In the men's Premier League 2024–25, who came third?

A. Aston Villa

B. Chelsea

C. Newcastle

D. Manchester City

23 In their climactic match of 2024 to West Ham, how many goals did Liverpool score?

A. 5

B. 3

C. 7

D. 4

24 Before the 2024–25 season, which was the last season where Liverpool won the Premier League trophy?

A. 2011–12

B. 2022–23

C. 2016–17

D. 2019–20

25 What number does Alexander Isak have for Newcastle United?
   A. 14
   B. 21
   C. 7
   D. 28

26 Which Chelsea boss bid farewell to her team at the end of the 2023–24 season?
   A. Natalia Arroyo
   B. Emma Hayes
   C. Sonia Bompastor
   D. Marc Skinner

27 And who replaced her?
   A. Matt Beard
   B. Rehanne Skinner
   C. Sonia Bompastor
   D. Amandine Miquel

28 How many goals did Barcelona score across all competitions in the 2024–25 season?
A. 152
B. 174
C. 180
D. 124

29 In the 2024–25 season, who became the youngest player to score 50 times in the Premier League?
A. Jude Bellingham
B. Lamine Yamal
C. Kylian Mbappé
D. Bukayo Saka

30 Which WSL player below is a goal keeper for Aston Villa?
A. Janine Leitzig
B. Sabrina D'Angelo
C. Emma Byrne
D. Lize Kop

31 In the 2023–24 season, how many goals did Alexander Isak score in the Premier League?

A. 10
B. 19
C. 25
D. 21

32 What team does Myles Lewis-Skelly play for in the 2024–25 season?

A. Arsenal
B. AC Milan
C. Barcelona
D. Real Madrid

33 What is Newcastle United FC's nickname?

A. The Magpies
B. The Ravens
C. The Eagles
D. The Seagulls

34 Who is the goal keeper for Barcelona in 2024–25 WSL?

A. Ann-Katrin Berger

B. Lydia Williams

C. Cata Coll

D. Hannah Hampton

35 Who scored a whopping 34 goals and 25 assists across 57 games for Barcelona?

A. Harry Kane

B. Lamine Yamal

C. Raphinha

D. Alexander Isak

36 Who is the manager for Arsenal?

A. David Moyes

B. Unai Emery

C. Neil Adams

D. Mikel Arteta

37 Which team had Lucy Bronze transferred to this year?

A. Manchester City
B. Chelsea
C. Lyon
D. Barcelona

38 What is Arsenal team's nickname?

A. The Gunners
B. The Reds
C. The Hammers
D. The Toffees

39 Which WSL player had won 25 trophies in 10 years at Barcelona before moving to Arsenal?

A. Aitana Bonmati
B. Mariona Caldentey
C. Ona Batlle
D. Patri Guijarro

40 Who below is a goal keeper for Man City in WSL?
A. Hannah Hampton
B. Phallon Tullis-Joyce
C. Ayaka Yamashita
D. Rachael Laws

41 Which team to Matz Sels move to in one of the top signings of the season?
A. AC Milan
B. Liverpool
C. Manchester City
D. Nottingham Forest

42 Who did Eberechi Eze and Jean-Philippe Mateta play for in the 2025–25 season?
A. Tottenham Hotspur
B. Chelsea
C. AFC Wimbledon
D. Crystal Palace

43 Which team is Eddie Howe manager for?
A. Manchester United
B. Arsenal
C. Bournemouth
D. Newcastle United

44 Who was Jürgen Klopp's replacement as manager of Liverpool?
A. Eddie Howe
B. Thomas Frank
C. Marco Silva
D. Arne Slot

45 In the Scottish Premiership Champions Group, how many points did Celtic have at the end?
A. 92
B. 89
C. 70
D. 100

46 Who was the Liverpool captain for the 2024–25 season?
A. Wataru Endo
B. Mohamed Salah
C. Virgil van Dijk
D. Milos Kerkez

47 An 'El Clasico' match is between what two teams?
A. Manchester City and Manchester United
B. Real Madrid and Barcelona
C. Bayern Munich and AC Milan
D. Arsenal and Chelsea

48 Before the 2024–25 season, what year was the last time Newcastle won a domestic trophy?
A. 1951   C. 1966
B. 1970   D. 1955

49 How many goals did Cole Palmer score in the Chelsea – Brighton match in the first half?
A. 2   C. 1
B. 4   D. 3

50 What is Liverpool FC's nickname?
A. The Reds   C. The Walkers
B. Pool Sharks   D. The Bees

WORDSEARCH

Find the teams and player names in the word search below!
They can be horizontal, vertical, diagonal and backwards.

G	K	B	O	N	M	A	T	I	V	U	T	E
C	E	A	N	E	W	C	A	S	T	L	E	A
H	K	X	S	O	J	A	J	F	L	I	D	L
E	H	J	B	I	G	O	A	L	W	V	S	L
L	W	C	R	U	W	R	W	C	B	E	V	I
S	R	D	O	H	Q	Y	S	A	E	R	Y	V
E	L	A	N	E	S	R	A	L	F	P	E	N
A	R	F	Z	U	E	J	K	M	U	O	U	O
M	L	P	E	E	G	A	A	Y	A	O	G	T
H	K	A	N	E	V	T	W	E	F	L	A	S
T	R	C	H	A	M	P	I	O	N	S	E	A
S	U	I	G	R	E	M	L	A	P	E	L	Q

LIVERPOOL   SAKA   ISAK
ARSENAL   KANE   BONMATI
CHELSEA   BRONZE   CHAMPIONS
NEWCASTLE   YAMAL   GOAL
ASTON VILLA   PALMER   LEAGUE

DESIGN YOUR OWN KIT

What's your favourite football kit? Maybe it's the one your team plays in. Maybe you've always secretly admired the one your rivals play in. Or maybe it's a combination nobody's ever seen before…

Now's the chance to design your perfect kit. Plain? Stripes? Hoops? Patterns? Polka dots? It's up to you. We've even given you an extra blank kit so you can make an away strip!

FOOTBALL BINGO

BACK OF THE NET	THEY NEED SPACE!	IN THE BOX	THEY NEED TO CHANGE THINGS UP
IT'S OVER!	IT'S ON TARGET	HE GOT A HAND ON IT	EARLY DOORS
GETTING STUCK IN!	BEAUTIFUL CROSS	THE REF WANTS A WORD	HE'S GOT TO HIT THE TARGET FROM HERE!
FINISH WHAT THEY STARTED	HE GETS IN BEHIND	IT'S ONE-ON-ONE	THEY'RE PICKING UP THE PACE

The next time you're watching the beautiful game, play along with the bingo cards below! There are two cards, so you can grab a friend and play against each other. Cross off the footie phrase when you hear it from one of the commentators. First one to get four in a row wins!

WHAT A GOAL!	THAT WILL BE A CORNER	LOOKING FOR AN OPENING	PARKING THE BUS
THEY'VE WOKEN UP	SHOWING A LOT OF PROMISE	WHAT A SAVE!	LET'S SEE THE REPLAY OF THAT
OFF THE POST!	LOST POSSESSION	BEAUTIFUL BALL	HE HAS SPACE
IT'S A FAST KICK	THEY'RE CATCHING THEIR BREATH	THE REF WANTS TO CHECK SOMETHING	NO ONE CAN CATCH HIM

ANSWERS

ANAGRAMS

Lucy Bronze	C L Boy run ez
Keira Walsh	I W Real Kash
Lauren James	Nue Lame Jars
Renee Sleger	See Ergel Ren
Mayre Ramirez	Marem I Rez Ray
Sandy Baltimore	More Salt Bin Day
Frida Maanum	If A Man A Druma
Alessia Russo	A Sassio Rules
Chloe Kelly	Leechy Lock
Melchie Dumornay	Melodic Human Rye
Mariona Caldentey	Italy Romance Dane
Beth Mead	Bad Theme

QUIZ

1) C, 2) D, 3) C, 4) D, 5) C, 6) A, 7) A, 8) D, 9) C,
10) C, 11) D, 12) C, 13) A, 14) C, 15) B, 16) D,
17) B, 18) B, 19) D, 20) C, 21) A, 22) D, 23) A, 24) D,
25) A, 26) B, 27) C, 28) B, 29) D, 30) B, 31) D, 32) A,
33) A, 34) C, 35) C, 36) D, 37) B 38) A, 39) B, 40) C,
41) D, 42) D, 43) D, 44) D, 45) A, 46) C,
47) B, 48) D, 49) B, 50) A

HOW DID YOU DO IN THE QUIZ?

1 – 10	Footie Rookie
11 – 20	Rising Star
21 – 30	Player of the Match
31 – 40	Top Baller
41 – 50	Ultimate Football Hero

WORDSEARCH

```
G  K  B  O  N  M  A  T  I  V  U  T  E
C  E  A  N  E  W  C  A  S  T  L  E  A
H  K  X  S  O  J  A  J  F  L  I  D  L
E  H  J  B  I  G  O  A  L  W  V  S  L
L  W  C  R  U  W  R  W  C  B  E  V  I
S  R  D  O  H  Q  Y  S  A  E  R  Y  V
E  L  A  N  E  S  R  A  L  F  P  E  N
A  R  F  Z  U  E  J  K  M  U  O  U  O
M  L  P  E  E  G  A  A  Y  A  O  G  T
H  K  A  N  E  V  T  W  E  F  L  A  S
T  R  C  H  A  M  P  I  O  N  S  E  A
S  U  I  G  R  E  M  L  A  P  E  L  Q
```

CAN'T GET ENOUGH OF ULTIMATE FOOTBALL HEROES?

Check out heroesfootball.com
for quizzes, games, and competitions!

Plus join the Ultimate Football Heroes
Fan Club to score exclusive content and
be the first to hear about
new books and events.
heroesfootball.com/subscribe/